Created for Communion *with* God

The Promise of Genesis 1 & 2

Created for Communion *with* God

The Promise of Genesis 1 & 2

Harrison Perkins

LEXHAM PRESS

Created for Communion with God: The Promise of Genesis 1 & 2

Lexham Press, 1313 Commercial St., Bellingham, WA 98225
LexhamPress.com

Print ISBN 9781683597643
Digital ISBN 9781683597650
Library of Congress Control Number 2024943855

Lexham Editorial: Todd Hains, Andrew Sheffield, Katrina Smith, Mandi Newell
Cover Design: Lydia Dahl
Typesetting: ProjectLuz.com

24 25 26 27 28 29 30 / US / 12 11 10 9 8 7 6 5 4 3 2 1

For the elders with whom I've served on sessions who give extraordinary service to Christ's church

*at Oakland Hills Community Church (OPC)—
John Frith, Mark Hakim, Mark Rebhan, and Greg Weigler*

*and at London City Presbyterian Church—
Dick Haffenden, Andy Longwe, Adam De Jong,
Gabriel Amorim, and Bob Akroyd*

brothers in the gospel, co-laborers in our vineyard, treasured friends

CONTENTS

PRAYER TO THE MAKER OF HEAVEN & EARTH

I lift up my eyes to the hills.
From where does my help come?
My help comes from the Lord,
who made heaven and earth.
Psalm 121:1–2

Almighty Father, you are the Maker of heaven and earth. Yet by our sin, by our fears, by our unbelief, we act as if the world is ours rather than yours. We so easily look more at your creation than to you, our Creator, exchanging the glory of the eternal God for that which our hands might fashion. Lift our eyes, O Lord, and refresh us with your glorious majesty that we might be captivated by the great breadth of your splendor. By your Word show us the light of your countenance and we shall be whole. We pray you hear us because of Christ, Amen.

AN INVITATION TO COMMUNION

Creation & Contemplating the Creator

The book of Genesis continually captures the church's imagination, captivating our thoughts with its description of the origins of the entire universe and, all the more, our own species. We seem never to tire of revisiting what details about our beginnings or even our modern world we might pull from the canon's opening narrative. Truly, our ongoing fascination with a short two or three chapters in the Bible shows how God has inspired the holy Scripture with inexhaustible riches.

Because the Scripture is primarily about God, our continued focus should perpetually unearth new riches about the Lord in his majesty. Our explorations into what Genesis 1–2 may teach about creation itself represent efforts to take the Bible seriously concerning every facet of God's world. Still, we cannot let ourselves become so preoccupied with themes about creation that we neglect what the Bible says about the Creator.

The studies in this book emphasize the doctrine of God in Genesis 1–2, hoping to accentuate the creation story's properly theological aspects. Truly, Genesis records genuine history. The purpose of that history is to teach us about God himself and our relationship with him. Wherever you may be among various positions concerning the creation week, the conclusions offered in this book are meant to be an agreeable baseline that expands on how Genesis points us above the created world to consider God's transcendent glory.

The hope for these studies is that they provide encouragement for your soul, grounded in the biblical text, moving to truly theological reflections, and always culminating in how each passage of Scripture points us to the Lord Jesus Christ as our Savior. Sometimes Bible studies can be intensely scientific, in two senses. First, we can be intensely scientific in studying the Scripture by examining the text's minute details at length, doing extensive word studies, grammatical analysis, and literary evaluation. Second, specifically concerning Genesis, we can be intensely scientific by focusing on what the Bible teaches about science.

The Bible should make us appreciate other things, too. In the fourteenth century, an important discussion took place about the value of beauty in thinking about God. The Renaissance scholar Petrarch wrote, "One may almost say that theology actually is poetry, poetry concerning God."[1] Petrarch's colleague Giovanni Boccaccio reinforced this sentiment, writing, "Theology is nothing less than the poetry of God."[2] These poets thought that theology, whatever else it can accomplish in teaching us about the scientific disciplines, must move people as they think about God by having an element of beauty, an affective component, so that it is poetry about God.

This prompts us to consider what beauty is, since it will remain a theme throughout these studies. Often, our first impulse when we try to define an idea is to find the word in the dictionary. But our understanding of "beauty" would seem a bit anemic if we were to reach for such a clinical tool to describe what we mean. Our purpose in reflecting on Genesis to find a poetic theology goes beyond breaking down the text's components in a scientific way, although not excluding that, to recognize how we are moved to appreciate our communion with God as pleasing to our souls. So, we will consider beauty as that which strikes us as pleasing and desirable, hoping that our reflections on Genesis will help us to comprehend life in communion with God as beautiful.

However far short they may fall of being poetic, these studies intend to set your attention on God to stir up your soul to a joyful consideration of the One who made you. They focus emphatically on moving quickly to theological reflections, drawing out the implications for our lives, always driving the point toward our relationship with God. Given that God is the divine author of the Bible, these investigations take for granted that he inspired the Scripture with rich meaning that always points to Christ as the Savior, who is the scope and hope of all Scripture (Luke 24:27). These theological expositions, therefore, always end by drawing attention to the Lord Jesus and our hope for salvation in him. In this way, they invite us into communion with God by exploring how he formed us for relationship with him, looking at the universe's first extraordinary days.

CRAFTED FOR COMMUNION

Beginning to Study the Beginning

God made you to know him. God is at the heart of the Christian faith, since he created humanity to experience him, glorify him, and enjoy him throughout our lives. God is the all-encompassing reality that should captivate the attention of every person—even more, every believer in Christ. God, who eternally lives as Father, Son, and Spirit in perfect communion with one another, has embedded in the fabric of creation the possibility for creatures to participate in communion with him as well. Our eternal Maker is love itself, abounding in so much love that he found it fitting to form creatures outside himself so that there might be other beings to experience and enjoy his overflowing love.

God inspired the holy Scriptures so that we might know about him and how to relate to him. God gave us the Bible as an interface for our relationship with him. In his Word, God gives us his very self. The Bible is not a magic book, as if reading it is an incantation that causes other good things to happen to us throughout the day, but it is a miraculous book in that God himself delivered its words to his people through human authors, providentially preserving the inerrant text across the centuries, so that everyone who has access to this book might know who the true God is and the wonderful things that he has done for his people. Moreover, the Bible is miraculous because in the very action of reading its words, we have communion with God as we learn about him, come to know him more, and have our faith increased. The Bible does not magically produce *other* blessings in our lives but miraculously itself *is* the blessing of providing communion with God. Scripture makes Christ truly present with us.[1]

For these reasons, confessional churches have long called the Bible a *means of grace*. The Word functions as a means of grace as God uses Scripture as a creaturely tool—creaturely meaning simply that it belongs to the created universe rather than to God's own essence—to bring about spiritual effects. Like a carpenter uses a hammer to drive a nail into a board, so God uses his holy Word to bring unbelieving hearts to faith and to grow believers in trust, assurance, and holiness. In this respect, Westminster Larger Catechism question 155 provides a beautiful summary of this truth:

> How is the Word made effectual to salvation?
>
> The Spirit of God makes the reading, but especially the preaching of the Word, an effectual means of enlightening, convincing and humbling sinners; of driving them out of themselves, and drawing them unto Christ; of conforming them to His image, and subduing them to His will; of strengthening them against temptations and corruptions; of building them up in grace, and establishing their hearts in holiness and comfort through faith unto salvation.[2]

In other words, God's Word is powerful because it draws us into a relationship with God, preserves and strengthens us in that relationship, and equips us to live for God in the world.

You might be wondering what this point about the means of grace and our relationship with God has to do with Genesis 1–2. In truth, everything. Even from Scripture's opening words, our attention is on God: "In the beginning, *God* … ." The Bible's first point focuses your sight on God. Its continued focus throughout every page remains to draw you more deeply into that heart-warming, life-giving, world-changing consideration of the God who made the universe and who made you to know him.

This book's purpose, therefore, is to remind us about the riches of Genesis 1–2 for reflecting on our relationship with the Lord. It emphasizes how the Scripture's first statement—"In the beginning, *God* … "—begins with a point intended to captivate you with your Maker's incredible majesty, pulling you into communion with him within one phrase, that then traces out across the remainder of the Scripture, including particularly Genesis 1–2 and its account of how God made the universe and made us to have a relationship with him. This book is about how Genesis should invigorate, inspire, and increase your relationship with God.

COMING TO CONSIDER GENESIS

It's not too much to say that in the last 150 years, one of the more controversial issues for the Christian church has concerned the phrase "ordinary days" in reference to the length of the creation week.[3] In light of the world's increasingly popular appeals to science as an alternative to Christian faith, believers have understandably spent a tremendous amount of time thinking about what the Scripture teaches concerning the main issues about which modern science claims to have sure knowledge. One of our main problems has been understanding the earliest Genesis narratives, particularly in light of developing scientific theories about the origins of the universe and humanity. Regardless of how we might understand the days of Genesis 1 and their length in relation to modern science, these days are certainly not *ordinary*.

Genesis 1–2 describes *extraordinary* days in which the whole universe comes into existence and God works over the earth to make it fit for humanity to inhabit so that we might be his covenant creatures. Apart from our impulse to use language that pushes against what we often perceive as challenges to biblical truth, every Christian should find magnificent and indeed extraordinary days in the opening chapters of our Scripture. God does amazing things in the first chapters of the Bible and records them for us so that his covenant people might be encouraged, exhorted, and equipped to live our lives with and before our God. In other words, whatever we conclude about what Genesis 1–2 has to say about modern science, certainly these chapters have much to say about our communion with God.

Although Christians who have read the Bible for any length of time usually have specific questions that they want answered about Genesis 1, the reflections in this book intend to set aside those questions for the time being and to listen afresh to what these rich and wonderful chapters say about our relationship with God. Our thinking again about Genesis 1–2 through the thematic lens of *communion with God* will reclaim this portion of Scripture as being fundamentally about God and about the bearing that God intends his inspired Word to have on the way that we live with him. John Calvin comments on Genesis 1:6, "He who would learn astronomy, and other recondite arts, let him go elsewhere."[4] Likely, not all will agree about how thoroughly we should apply Calvin's statement, nor about how far Calvin himself would intend us to apply it. Regardless, we should all agree that that Genesis is first about theology, and therefore our communion with God, before it is about issues in the physical sciences. God inspired the book of Genesis to have the pointed purpose of addressing his people as we relate to him in our walk with him. Even the first chapters of Genesis are loaded with theological riches that tell us about God and what it means to be creatures in communion with him.

This first chapter establishes the simple point that we need to read Genesis foremost as God's people who are longing to hear about our God. None of these considerations are meant to disparage attempts to reconcile Genesis and science, but they are designed to calibrate our interests to be more about the Creator than the creation. Sinners—even redeemed sinners—so easily become overly obsessed with ourselves, finding ways to justify the thoughts that most entertain us. Ironically, those thoughts are also usually about us. Yet Genesis 1–2 gives us the opportunity to look beyond ourselves to the God who called us into being. As those made in God's image, we are uniquely able among God's creatures to lift our heads above what is directly before us to look to the horizon to consider how we relate to our Maker. Although firmly tied to our natural world and thoroughly part of it, we alone among the creatures are also ordered for the supernatural end of communion with God. We alone are able to raise our heads and gaze upward above the natural order toward that blessed fellowship with the Almighty God.[5] It is fitting that God's Word, even as it describes God's work of making the world, should push our eyes above creation to the Creator.

A CALL TO COMMUNION

The rest of this chapter deepens the preceding considerations by exploring how we should think about the book of Genesis as a text inspired by God for his people's benefit. From the outset, then, a few things ought to focus the way we think about this text. The traditional and conservative position is that Moses was the fundamental author of Genesis–Deuteronomy. Assuming the Exodus took place around 1500 BC, Moses wrote Genesis–Deuteronomy sometime shortly after God brought Israel to Mount Sinai and covenanted with them. This fact may not seem terribly interesting but carries significance.

God inspired Genesis *as an address to his covenant people* to tell them about life with him. As he brought Israel out of slavery, God inspired this book to give them the historical prologue to the relationship he was formalizing with them at Sinai. Even Scripture's first book speaks directly to sinners as they encounter their Redeemer. The opening chapters of Genesis are not a geological treatise but describe the majesty of the God who made all things by the sheer power of his Word and who now invites us to come before him as people restored to a good relationship with him. Genesis speaks to God's covenant people about having communion with our Lord.[6]

Critically, Genesis is meant as a covenantal address to create, sanctify, and assure God's covenant people. God has always covenanted with humanity, establishing fixed and certain relationships with us. To put all those pieces together into a full picture of God's first covenant with us, this book takes time to unpack these passages as they confront us with an encounter with God one aspect at a time. Nonetheless, the scope of Genesis 1–2 drives us to consider fully how we have been in covenant with God since creation. God builds the universe as space for worship, a covenantal temple. We are made in his image, entailing our ethical obligation to show his goodness by acting in accordance with his character. God made us for everlasting communion with him, consecrating the Sabbath to mark the time for communion with him, then building the garden in Eden as the place for communion with him. These two aspects of ethical obligation and special communion with God characterize the basic features of God's covenantal relationship with Adam. These features also teach about how we are still meant to relate to God in the new covenant.

So Genesis is about knowing who God is and what his relationship with his covenant people is supposed to be, even from the first moments that the universe existed. God did not inspire this text as an address to the whole world. Even though this text records the beginning of the world, it was not written at the beginning of the world. It was written as God made a covenant with Israel at Mount Sinai as an address to his people. That Genesis is God's authoritative and inspired address to inform and direct his people in their relationship with him entails two applications for everything that we will consider together in this book.

First, given how often Christians feel on the defensive about Genesis 1–2, we too easily overlook that it speaks to us about how we are supposed to live with God. How many times have you heard "But science has disproved the Bible" as a response to your efforts to share the gospel with unbelieving friends? The pressure that we may feel from the world to explain ourselves concerning the world's origins trains us to think apologetically (meaning the practice of apologetics for defending the faith) about the content of the creation narrative. We risk beginning to think that we need to protect Genesis 1–2 from the world rather than trust God to make it and its meaning powerful unto salvation and sanctification.

The big takeaway from this application is that if you are a Christian, God intended Genesis to have a real bearing on *your* life before him. Admittedly, Moses did include polemical points within Genesis 1–2, wherein he intentionally challenged the creation narratives of other religions.[7] Specifically, Genesis 1–2 confronts what other religions teach about their *gods* by displaying the God of Israel as the only true God over the whole universe, who deserves all praise and worship. In other words, whereas we too readily see Genesis 1 as a rebuttal to what *other* people out there believe about *creation*, the account of our origins means to confront *everyone* with the truth about the *Creator*.

We might think about this point concerning the polemical value of Genesis by using the illustration of a layer cake. On the one hand, the cake's bottom layer represents the material world, meaning a focus on this layer includes describing features of creation like the earth's age or its physical makeup. On the other hand, the cake's top layer represents God's work as the one who is over and distinct from the created realm, entailing that this layer reveals supernatural truths concerning how God made the world and how he is the only true God. Too often, we let the world's interpretations and questions make us think that Genesis 1 is primarily about that bottom layer when truly it portrays the top.[8] The polemical thrust of Genesis, still relevant today, concerns what people think of God rather than the earth.

Second, since this book is an address to God's covenant people about our relationship with God, then our study even in the first chapters of this book must focus on God himself and our relationship with him. To put a fine point on this application, if we study Genesis with our attention more on the creation than on the Creator, then we have again fundamentally redirected, or perhaps even distorted, the meaning of God's Word. To highlight the world more than God is again to abuse these portions of Scripture.

Our big takeaway is to read Genesis like it matters for your everyday life as a Christian before God. This book is not fodder for debate but is about God's Word to his people. We observe that Genesis is about God, and therefore, we must read it for how God intended it to address his covenant people. Even as we may legitimately find material for discussion about defending our faith against opponents, we cannot let that displace Genesis as foundationally about encouraging our faith within the church as those in communion with God. Genesis is first and primarily relevant for those who would want to know how to have a relationship with the true God of the universe.

These reflections on Genesis 1–2 are, consequently, unashamedly theological. They are not meant to overturn any other studies of Genesis but are meant to provide spiritual nourishment for people who want to know what the Scripture says about our Triune God. For example, as we see God's power in rolling out the universe, in hanging the stars, and giving the earth a sustainable ecosystem so that we might live on it, we should be moved to think about how generous, caring, and kind God is in the ways he uses his power for his people. We should look most at the comfort we find in belonging to the almighty God who cares for us. God and our communion with God as his people is the heart of Genesis 1–2.

These reflections are, further, unashamedly Christ-centered. The underlying conviction is that when the resurrected Christ began "with *Moses* and all the Prophets [and] interpreted to them in all the Scriptures the things concerning himself," he knew exactly what he was doing and had infallible insight into the true and full meaning of all Scripture (Luke 24:27). Since Christ explained how the books that Moses wrote are about him, then we should search out that Christ-centered relevance. Since it was "*Jesus*, who saved a people out of the land of Egypt," we know that Christ was involved as Savior even in the events that Moses recorded (Jude 5). Since "the Rock was Christ" from which the Israelites drank spiritual nourishment as they traversed the wilderness, we know that Christ provided for his people's good during the ministry of Moses. Most pointedly for our considerations, Christ's preeminence shines in how "by him all things were created, in heaven and on earth, visible and invisible, whether thrones or dominions or rulers or authorities—all things were created through him and for him" (Colossians 1:17). So, we follow the apostles in understanding all Scripture, including Genesis 1–2, to teach us about the Lord Jesus. Each of our reflections, therefore, draws an explicit connection to how Genesis informs not merely our communion with God but even more specifically how sinners have communion with God through salvation in Christ.

CONCLUSION

We live in the digital age when data is the chief capital. The collection, storage, and transfer of information are the primary commodities of our day. Yet there is something nice about sitting next to someone you love, saying nothing but enjoying their presence. This presence makes our hearts even happier than learning something new.

Too quickly we conclude Genesis 1–2 is about conveying information when it is truly crafted for communion. The teaching in this creation account is not so much a data dump as a love letter. This narrative of how God fashioned the universe should lock your attention not onto the facets of creation as much as on how God summoned you into being so that he could care for you. In this way, this text is a means of grace for God's people, intended for making God present in our lives and increasing our faith in what he has done for us in Christ. The Scripture is inexhaustible in its riches, always offering new and fertile nutrients, because God gives himself to us in words of holy writ crafted for communion.

QUESTIONS FOR FURTHER REFLECTION

1. What is Genesis primarily about?
2. How does Scripture's very purpose help us to see God's desire to have communion with his people?

3. In what ways do the biblical narratives become more exciting to you when you see God's Word as a means of grace rather than only a historical record?

4. Why is Genesis important for the ordinary Christian life, not just for apologetic discussions?

THE BEGINNING OF COMMUNION

The Creator & the Created

Since Genesis addresses God's people about their relationship with God, then it also tells us about the beginning of our relationship with God as the creatures made in his image. Now, this relationship begins because in creation, God called into existence what did not previously exist. A relationship requires two *distinct* parties. In regard to our communion with our Creator God, Genesis teaches precisely that the Creator is the eternal God who called creation into existence and made a relationship with creatures in it. Therefore, God remains thoroughly distinct from the creature even though he has forged a relationship with us.

Genesis 1:1–2 has been traditionally understood to recount the absolute beginning of the universe. That beginning, however, marks some fundamental and amazing truths about God and how we relate to him. These verses read:

> At the beginning, God created the heavens and the earth. Now, the earth lacked form and was void, and

> darkness was over the face of the deep, and the Spirit of God was hovering over the face of the waters.[1]

As the opening words of Scripture record the first moments of the physical universe, they help us understand some crucial things about God and our relationship—our communion—with him. This chapter's main point is that Genesis 1:1–2 addresses God's people to remember that God is entirely different from us, which ought to fill us with hope and wonder.

GOD'S FIRST ACT OF CREATION

The Bible's first two verses contain and highlight some of the most exciting and deepest theology that we could ever consider. However, Bible interpreters have understood verses 1–2 in a few different ways, so before teasing out these verses' rich theological significance, we need to consider what they mean.

Some interpreters have understood these verses as a summary statement of the whole series of creation events, covering everything that happens through Genesis 2:3. To illustrate, imagine that I say to you, "I had an amazing day today. First, I had a delicious breakfast; then, I had lots of fun at work; and last, it was good to get home." In this story, "I had an amazing day today" is an overview of the whole story that is about to follow. That first sentence encapsulates all the events that compose the real narrative of the story. Some have understood "At the beginning, God created the heavens and the earth" in the same way.[2]

This understanding entails that this first statement about God creating the heavens and the earth does not describe a distinct act unto itself but introduces the story about God's creative work that takes places throughout the rest of the story. For this reason, many interpreters who hold this view would prefer to translate verses 1–2, "When God began to create the heavens and the earth, the earth was without form and void."[3] This translation suggests that as God began his creative work, the earth was already there, but it simply had no form and was empty.[4] In this case, the Bible assumes that God created by using physical matter that was already present. Some interpreters who understand verse 1 this way still affirm that God created the physical universe but say that their view implies that Genesis does not reveal how the material of creation came into existence.[5] Further, God may have been interacting with pre-existing, even eternal, physical matter. Regardless, this interpretation understands the narrative in Genesis to make no comment on the origins of the physical universe. However, another interpretation better fits the grammar and theology of Genesis 1.

The better interpretation understands God's work of creating the heavens and the earth as the first distinct act that God performed in making the universe. This distinct act takes place before the main thrust of the narrative really gets going with the events of day one in verse 3.[6] To illustrate this interpretation through another version of that imagined conversation, the story would now run: "I woke up today, had a delicious breakfast, then ... " In this telling, "I woke up" clearly functions as the first event of my amazing day. This sense is the way we should understand Genesis 1:1.

The Bible's first sentence then describes the actual beginning of the universe as God called it into being. The translation provided above, "*At* the beginning, God created the heavens and the earth," is not meant as a mutually exclusive alternative to the standard "*in* the beginning" but simply highlights theologically that this event of creation is the first moment of the universe. In the traditional understanding of this verse, although it is very difficult for our minds to comprehend, neither space nor time existed before God's act recounted in verse 1.

I used to love going to the movies. There was always one moment between the trailers and the film that was most effective for building real excitement. After the final preview, the sound went quiet, the screen dimensions adjusted to the right ratio for this movie, and the lights got even darker. In that still moment, you were ready, and then ... BAM! The screen roared to life again and launched you into the story you'd been waiting to see. Genesis 1:1 is supposed to have that effect, bringing us to the moment when we are ready to be launched into the story. Genesis 1:1 marks the first event, functioning as the dimming of the lights for dramatic effect to put us in the right posture for the story that God is about to unfold in his Word.

We ought to have an excitement about God's Word. Genesis 1:1 is about putting you on edge for the most exciting story that you could ever hear: the story of God's redemptive history. At the church I pastor, I purposefully make a big deal out of the public reading of Scripture (1 Timothy 4:13). In our services, we stand when holy Scripture is read aloud. I tend to leave long pauses between announcing the text, asking them to stand, and then stating with as much resolution as I can muster, "This is God's Word," followed by reading the text. I want to make the point that something serious, something special, something eventful is about to happen. That something is that God's own address to his covenant people is about to be heard. I want the buildup to be as profound as we can manage. Genesis 1:1 is Scripture's own contribution to that sort of effect. God just made everything, so we should buckle up for what happens next.

In this understanding, Genesis 1:2 then picks up the movie by describing the earth in its initial state *as the result of* God's creative work in verse 1. I have translated it, "Now, the earth lacked form and was void, and darkness was over the face of the deep, and the Spirit of God was hovering over the face of the waters." In this rendering, "now" draws attention to how the Hebrew grammar shifts attention from the wide scope of the entire universe to focus specifically on the earth for the following narrative. We might think of another imaginary story that goes like this: "The whole buffet at the restaurant was sprawling and full of wonderful foods. Now, the steak in particular was delightful." This story changes from a wide-angle lens to a narrow-angle focus. So, too, Genesis 1:2 shifts attention from the panoramic perspective on how God brought the whole universe into existence to zoom in on the further creative works that he was about to do concerning the earth in particular.

In this case, God created the heavens and the earth, and when he did, the earth's initial state was that it lacked form and was empty. That condition sets the stage for how God will develop the earth's state throughout the rest of the creation narrative. In sum, the crucial point is that the events of verses 1–2 occur emphatically before day one of creation begins in verse 3. This first event tells us that God made all the physical matter of the universe.[7] With that in mind, we can now unpack some of the rich theological significance that this understanding entails.

GOD IS DIFFERENT FROM US

There is a fundamental distinction between the Creator and the creation that is underscored by the Bible's description of how God made the universe. God is different and distinct from the universe and everything in it. As Joel Beeke and Paul Smalley succinctly state, "the Bible knows only two categories of being: God and what God made."[8] How could it be otherwise, since God brought everything that is not God into existence?

God's power is on full display and is an intended emphasis throughout the creation narrative. Although in other places in the creation account God "forms" aspects of creation (יָצַר, *yatsar*),

God's first act was to "create" (בָּרָא, *bara'*). The difference between these two verbs highlights that God did not make the universe by using preexistent matter but brought everything in the universe into being.[9] So there was no physical matter of any sort or any of the dimensions that belong to creation before God brought the heavens and earth into existence. Further, the spiritual realms, which we often call heaven, did not exist before God created them either. So the first act of creation brought the earth, the physical heavens, and the spiritual heavens along with the angels into existence (Job 38:4–7; Psalm 104:2–5).[10] God's power is manifest in how he did not need anything to make the universe, creating it simply by his own word and depending on nothing.[11]

God's power is obvious in how he made such a multivalent creation, not composed of only one type of existence. Although some doubt that "the heavens and the earth" refers to God's creation of the distinct spiritual and material realms, Psalm 148 seemingly confirms that this distinction was at least partially in view.[12] This psalm falls into two parts, summoning the heavens to praise God in verses 1–6 and the earth to praise him in verses 7–12, clearly structuring this extended call to worship around the opening lines of Genesis. Admittedly, the first section about the heavens includes the sun, moon, and stars, excluding a neat and tidy distinction between the heavens and the earth as spiritual and material realms. Nonetheless, the psalmist's first call to worship is:

> Praise the Lord from the heavens;
> praise him in the heights!
> Praise him, all his angels;
> praise him, all his hosts! (Psalm 148:1–2)

The psalmist's address to *the angels* under the call to the heavens to praise God indicates that the heavens *include* the spiritual realm where angels reside, as it would in Genesis 1:1, even if later references to the heavens encompass celestial bodies of the material universe. The second summons in this call to worship then addresses the earth:

> Praise the LORD from the earth,
> you great sea creatures and all deeps,
> fire and hail, snow and mist,
> stormy wind fulfilling his word!
> Mountains and all hills,
> fruit trees and all cedars!
> Beasts and all livestock,
> creeping things and flying birds!
> Kings of the earth and all peoples,
> princes and all rulers of the earth!
> Young men and maidens together,
> old men and children! (Psalm 148:7–12)

This summons to the earth includes not only sea creatures, birds, and livestock but also even fruit trees, representing the high point of vegetation from Genesis 1:11–13. Most crucially, it addresses the kings of the earth, specifically "men and maidens together," both indicating how this call to worship includes humanity as the pinnacle of the earthly realm and hinting at the royal role that humanity serves as God's image bearers called to rule over creation to God's glory—a theme we will explore later at more length. This psalm closes with a declaration of God's universal glory and his commitment to his people:

> Let them praise the name of the LORD,
> for his name alone is exalted;
> his majesty is above earth and heaven.
> He has raised up a horn for his people,
> praise for all his saints,

for the people of Israel who are near to him.
Praise the LORD! (Psalm 148:13–14)

The Lord's majesty is over earth and heaven, the two realms created in Genesis 1:1, and he continues to execute the same power he used in creation to bring hope to his people.

From its very first sentence, as later Scripture confirms, the Bible focuses on God and his works, especially his power and authority.[13] The creation narrative emphasizes God and his power, exemplifying a compressed instance of how the whole Scripture operates. God's power is further underscored through his commands that shape and develop the creation and even through the order in which they are portrayed. The Scripture describes the order of creation as light coming before the sun and moon (Genesis 1:3, 14–15). A worldly perspective believes that God is dependent on the operations of the world for what he can and cannot do. As John Calvin diagnosed, we are most prone "to tie down the power of God to those instruments, the agency of which he employs."[14] Although God normally works through ordinary means, Genesis makes the theological point that he certainly does not need them to achieve his purposes.[15] Since the other cultures of Israel's day often considered the sun and moon to be deities, the Scripture resoundingly declares that the true God is high above all the other perceived gods in both majesty and power. Those created things which others worship as gods were created by the true God.

Have you ever noticed how most stories about the virtue of strength feature a character who is set apart from all the rest? While coming-of-age stories can trace the main character's learning process, films about raw heroism usually center on the single most highly trained operative, the most elite agent, the most experienced treasure hunter—you get the idea. Apart from the comedy genre, I would hardly be interested in a story about a new dope bound for failure and untested in his skills. There is a mystery and allure about the figure set apart in might and ability. We need to realize that the true God dwarfs everything we could ever imagine about any of our heroes, or even what people have invented about false gods. God stands alone as the raw encapsulation of power and ability.

That God brought forth the universe simply by his own power underscores how he is distinct from the creation. Nothing existed before he made it, so all things owe their being to him. Far from being an arcane philosophical point, this underscores God's supreme majesty. God did not need anything to make the universe what it is now. God created out of nothing. This phrase "out of nothing" (*ex nihilo*) is something that Christians should know well. God created *out of nothing*. One of our core beliefs about God is captured and upheld in the simple phrase "out of nothing." (If I am sounding repetitive, it is because I want this phrase to be lodged in your memory.)

The doctrine of creation *ex nihilo* teaches us more about God than about creation itself. It points to God's incommunicable attribute of *aseity*. God's aseity means that he has life in and from himself. While every creature in some way or other derives its existence from an outside source—at least in the sense that we all have a beginning stemming from two parents conceiving us—God alone is underived. He is dependent on nothing, needs nothing, and comes from nothing. He is the original of all being, having no beginning, no source, and no foundation. God himself is the only fount of all being.

The beauty of God's aseity for the Christian life is that God does not need you. This truth has two rich applications. First, believer, you should know that since God does not need you, it means that he *wants* you. He is not dependent on you to give him anything that he lacks. So, you exist and are in relationship with him out of the sheer self-produced joy that God had in making you and bringing you to himself. Second, we should take great comfort, especially in our weaknesses, from the reality that God is not dependent on us for anything. That God never needs to lean on us means that we can always lean on him. So often, we limit our hopes about God's care for us and answered prayers to the ways we know that ultimately, we could come through for ourselves. God is not bound by our limitations, though. God does not need our strength to accomplish his purposes or even to meet the needs that we ourselves have. God is able above and beyond our highest capacities because of his aseity. We take heart in our weaknesses that God can outshine us, being in no way dependent on us but ready and willing to pour forth his font of life and strength to bless his people.[16]

The doctrine of creation out of nothing also distinguishes the Christian understanding of the world from all others. The flipside of God's aseity is creation's dependence. What you think of the other events in the creation story *might* have bearing on the way Christians need to look at the world, but verses 1–2 are fundamental in thinking Christianly about the origins of the universe. Our conclusions here shape how we understand God's relationship to the creation. They mold our thought patterns either to highlight God as the eternally majestic, wholly transcendent and distinct *God* or to highlight creation as a paradigm into which God must fit himself.

The rest of Scripture confirms this interpretation that God created the universe out of nothing. In Hebrews 11:3, the writer explains: "By faith we understand that the universe was created by the word of God, so that what is seen was *not made out of things that are visible.*" Hebrews tells us that *by faith* we know that God brought the physical universe into existence from nothing, not needing to use anything that we can see today—since those things did not exist. As the medieval theologian Thomas Aquinas explains, although human reason cannot deduce that the universe had a beginning, we believe that truth because God's Word tells us so. He writes: "By faith alone do we hold, and by no demonstration can it be proved, that the world did not always exist, as was said above about the mystery of the Trinity."[17] Thomas, reflecting Hebrews, means that we receive and believe that the world had a definite beginning not because of human reason but because God's Word has revealed it. It is an *article of faith* rather than the product of a syllogism.

The apostle Paul further confirms the point that God made the universe out of nothing. He writes in Romans 4:17: "As it is written, 'I have made you the father of many nations'—in the presence of the God in whom he believed, who gives life to the dead and *calls into existence the things that do not exist.*" Paul's point is that there was a time when nothing existed except God alone. When God made the universe, he did so by calling things into existence rather than working with things that were already there. In other words, God did not depend on anything outside himself to create the world or the things that fill it. He made them out of nothing only by the fiat of his word.

This article of faith importantly distinguishes how Christians understand the world from how adherents to other religions and worldviews have often explained the universe's origins. All the way back to Greek philosophy and lingering into modern science, the assumption that the universe's physical material is eternal has captivated unbelieving thought. As Aristotle writes:

> For whichever substance or substances each thinker assumed to be primary he regarded as constituting the substantive existence of all things in general, all

> else being modifications, states, and dispositions of them. Any such ultimate substance they regarded as eternal (for they did not admit the transformation of elementary substances into each other), while they held that all else passed into existence and out of it endlessly.[18]

The belief is that the matter that composes the universe has always been here, even if it has perhaps looked different or been through various cycles. Modernity then shares paganism's belief that the physical parts of creation are eternal.

Science oversteps its bounds by commenting on God, since its job is to investigate the *natural* realm by repeatable, observable experiments. There is no repeatable, observable experiment that can prove that God does not exist, foremost because scientific experimentation cannot go past the bounds of nature. Only flawed reasoning concludes that only that which exists *like we do* can exist at all. After all, God is not contained in nature. He is supernatural. He made the material universe and enters into it but does not exist in the same way it does. God does not depend on anything for his existence, nor did he need anything to make the universe. He exists as Creator, whereas we exist as creatures.

In teaching that God created out of nothing, Scripture emphasizes something profound about God. The universe began at some point, and God was the one who made it. God, therefore, stands outside the physical universe and is not subject to our natural investigation. We cannot overcome the limitations of human finitude to climb into God's supernatural realm to inspect his essence. God remains transcendent, particularly as Creator.[19]

God's transcendence in the doctrine of creation out of nothing applies pastorally in two significant ways. First, it marks God's kindness and concern for us to know him. Precisely because we could not entirely reach him through our natural abilities, God has spoken to his people. We can know some things about God because of how he made the world to reveal himself to us naturally: "For his invisible attributes, namely, his eternal power and divine nature, have been clearly perceived, ever since the creation of the world, *in the things that have been made*" (Romans 1:20). Still, nature does not reveal everything we need to understand about God to know him properly, for example that the true God is Father, Son, and Spirit. In creation, he reveals himself in a certain limited way. In his special revelation, he makes himself known more clearly so that we might know him more fully, although still not exhaustively. He has addressed his people climactically in the Son and markedly by the Scriptures (Hebrews 1:1–2). What we could not investigate, God has told us. God is different from us, but we ought to rejoice that he has revealed something of himself to us. The Transcendent makes himself immanent by letting us know him through his revelation.

Second, creation out of nothing reminds us how powerful God is. Knowing that our God made everything we see by literally nothing but his own power makes our problems seem insignificant next to God's ability. These trials may weigh heavily on us but are no match for our God. We take hope that our God is able to remove our trials by his great power. If those trials linger, we trust that God is teaching us more about how to know him well since he is powerful enough to dispose of them quickly.[20]

GOD'S TIMELESS DEPENDABILITY

Another captivating implication of Genesis 1:1–2 is that God created not only physical matter but also time.[21] These verses reveal that God made time and space, further marking the Lord's transcendence. As creatures, you and I experience the passing of moments. Any of us who have taken a trip to the DMV and had to wait our turn to speak to the attendant who may or may not help us know the painful creak of passing seconds, reinforcing just how strapped to time we are. We must realize, however, that this experience is uniquely creaturely. *We* undergo the ticking of one second into the next, knowing the effects of one instant drifting by us into the past. God, on the other hand, is timeless and never changing. He does not experience the passage of time, and there is no succession of moments in his being. In this truth, taught concisely if implicitly in the opening words of Genesis, we again encounter the splendid majesty of the transcendent God. The Creator is not bound by the created.

Acknowledging that no creaturely explanation can ever fully capture the reality of God's attributes, an attempted illustration may still help us grasp at a limited understanding of God's timelessness. Imagine being at the football stadium before the game begins. As the stands are filling, music is playing to excite the crowd, and last preparations are being made. Somewhere in the stadium, there should be a scoreboard that has a timer to track the game's progression. At this point before the game has started, however, that timer is not ticking away the seconds. As you look at the field prior to the game's start, you know that time is not officially passing on that field. The clock is frozen for everything happening in the stadium. Moreover, that clock only progresses in reference to what happens concerning that game.

This illustration's point is that like the scoreboard's timer tracks seconds specifically concerning that game, *reality's* timer, the universal succession of moments, applies only to created things. Further, it did not start to count moments until God made the universe. There was no such thing as time "before" Genesis 1:1. The timer of creation does not apply to God, nor was there even such a thing as the passage of time until God brought the created universe into existence.

God's majesty is clearly displayed in his being outside time, his total lack of experiencing the succession of moments, his not entering into or passing through seasons, and his complete freedom from aging. In technical theology, we affirm that God alone is truly *eternal*, meaning that he does not experience time. We are *everlasting*, meaning that at least our souls never cease to experience an endless succession of moments, and believers will experience everlasting life. God, however, is not everlasting in that sense. He is eternal, different from us, as no time passes for or in God.

God's timeless transcendence has significant, soul-stirring relevance for your life. God's timelessness should deeply matter to you because his unchanging nature is the sure foundation of your hope and ability to trust God. To ground this more deeply, we need to understand the doctrine of God's *impassibility*, which teaches that God is not subject to emotional change. Sometimes, Christians who have never heard of impassibility or have not heard it explained properly find it odd, since the Bible is full of descriptions of God's love, wrath, patience, and so on. The key issue, however, is that impassibility denies that God's feelings *change*. God, including his feelings, cannot change because he is outside time. The passing of time is the necessary ingredient for change.

Let's illustrate—as best we, as creatures bound to time, can wrap our minds around God's timeless eternity—how we can affirm the biblical truth of God's love for his people and wrath for sin while also affirming that God's feelings do not change. Our lives develop like a movie, with each frame playing out one after the other as each moment of history ticks by. As we watch movies, we are moved to laugh as one scene develops or cry when another unfolds later. Because we experience history like a movie progresses, we struggle to think of God assessing history in any other manner. God, however, views history more like a comic book page than a movie. In a comic book, all the frames that tell the whole story are laid out at once and frozen in what each frame depicts. God views history not in progress, like a movie, but like a comic book, with history's every moment forever laid out as an eternal present before God. Nothing is past or future for the Lord. In this situation, God eternally and unchangeably has all love directed upon believers and all anger concentrated upon sin yet maintains this eternal disposition without change. Each moment remains always before God, and he always focuses the same disposition toward each state of affairs.

Although it has become popular to reject the doctrine of impassibility, preferring a description of God wherein his emotional life looks like ours, truly it is immensely good news that God does not shift in his feelings. God's impassibility means that his care for you in your moments of hurting will never pass away. God will not lose interest in your sufferings because he is eternally attentive to his people's needs for every moment of our existence. God's impassibility also means that his love is likewise immutable. Unlike our other relationships, in which feelings wax and wane for the other based on a host of factors, God's love for you is always perfect. On your best days, he does not love your more, nor could he. Conversely, on your worst days, he does not, and cannot, love you less. He is not subject to the ebbs and flows of a relationship as we experience them. All the more, whereas in our other relationships, "I'm fine" may mean truly fine or very angry, God's promises about his affection and care for you are always straightforward and dependable.

God's love for his people is fixed and certain. God will not, in fact cannot, change his mind about his love for you because, as James 1:17 says, God "does not change like shifting shadows." In the words of Geerhardus Vos, "the best proof that He will never cease to love us lies in that He never began."[22] Vos means that because God is timeless, there was never a moment within God's being "before" he was loving his people. Since God never changed from not loving you to loving you, and since he remains eternally immutable, he can never cease loving you. God's eternality and unchangingness mean that since God issued the gospel promise to Abraham, those who trust in his promises by faith will be rescued. It is impossible for that promise ever to be overturned.

CONCLUSION

We should be filled with hope and wonder because God is the Creator. The teaching of Genesis on creation makes clear that we are not God since he is different from and supreme to us. As Christians, this truth inspires us to be full of heart because we know the ultimate source of true comfort and delight. Where else might anyone run to find such security and dependability? The God who is beyond us has voluntarily condescended to know us, be with us, and make us his people.

For those of us living this side of humanity's swan dive into sin, there is inestimable comfort that God's gospel promise sounded out as far back as the moments right after Adam rebelled against God's law. When the Lord promised in Genesis 3:15 that the seed of the woman would crush the serpent's head, he declared that there would be a Savior to overcome the dire effects of sin's ruin. This promise pointed to the Lord Jesus Christ, who would be bruised by being crucified but nonetheless would destroy Satan and the stains of his work of luring Adam and Eve into sin.

All the more, because God is timeless, we have sure confidence in that promise. From the first ring of that gospel promise in Eden (Genesis 3:15), to that promise's formalization by covenant to Abraham (Genesis 15), to its fulfillment in the person and work of Jesus Christ (Revelation 12:9), God's unchanging nature has *guaranteed* it. God's transcendent and immutable nature upholds and secures our ability to know that sinners who flee to Christ by faith for rescue will be received into God's family. Our unchanging and sovereign God has promised it. Because of who God is, it is impossible for that promise to fail.

QUESTIONS FOR FURTHER REFLECTION

1. How did God create the universe?
2. What is the Creator-creature distinction?
3. What is the difference between natural and special revelation in how God reveals himself and what we can know of him?
4. How are we to understand God's eternality and his timeless dependability?
5. Why does God's impassibility bring the believer such comfort?

4 EFFECTIVE COMMUNION

God the Author of Order

Craftsmanship is pleasing when it performs to peak expectations. We love when things work well. If you were to hand-build a watch, you would have every reason to find great pleasure in a finely crafted finished product. Yet imagine that as you admire the handiwork of your new personally produced timepiece, you find the hands turning the wrong way. The disappointment would be magnified because your watch cannot do what you built it to do, namely, tell time accurately. You made this watch to fulfill a purpose but have found that it is not properly ordered to fulfill its purpose. A properly ordered watch has hands that turn clockwise and keep time, but a disordered watch is just dead weight. We build things with purpose, and properly ordered things fulfill their purpose.

The Genesis 1 narrative teaches us that God also creates things to be properly ordered to the specific purposes for which he made them. Throughout the creation story, God's act of bringing the universe into being and his successive works of shaping the features of the world all reveal that he built the creation to function properly. He designed specific features of the universe *with purpose* so that the cosmos operates with each piece working toward its appointed end.

God's purposeful design is not limited to the realm of nature alone but also summons humanity to specific responsibilities. As Genesis 1 teaches that God made humanity in his own image, we also see that this image-bearing function bears purpose for what our role is meant to be in the world. God purposefully designed us to be ordered to certain ends, so the creation narrative summons those who are made in God's image to fulfill our function. This chapter reflects on Genesis 1–2 to show the main point that God authored the world to have order and that people are meant to be ordered toward everlasting communion with God.

GOD'S PURPOSES

Although working through Scripture one verse at a time is necessary for some studies and highly fruitful for some portions of God's Word, some passages require a wider lens. Such is the case with Genesis 1 as we try to take in the scope of its teaching about how God brought the world to an inhabitable and functional state. As we look at the creation narrative to see its lessons about communion with God, we first need to see how God created the world with order that is meant to govern his people's lives. The result is that we have a structured environment in which to live out our relationship with the Lord.

To see the significance of how God works across the creation days, we need to note the earth's condition just after God brought it into existence. We considered already how "At the beginning, God created the heavens and the earth" reminds us that God brought the universe into existence out of nothing, using only his word, and that God is fundamentally distinct from the creation. We reflected on how verse 2—"Now the earth was without form and void, and darkness was over the face of the deep. And the Spirit of God was hovering over the face of the waters"—shows the earth's condition just after God created it, but the rest of the creation narrative is about God changing this condition in order to make the earth habitable, which culminates in the creation of humanity in God's image.[1] God's first act of creation, therefore, brought the heavens and the earth into existence but left the earth formless and empty, importantly marking the world's initial state as ugly, uninhabitable, and non-functional.[2]

God, however, had not finished his plans for his creation. The twofold "problem" that the earth was formless and void significantly shapes the creation narrative, informing how we ought to understand God's further creative works. In the first three days, God distinguished day and night, divided the waters that were above and below the expanse, and separated the land from the water, making the land sprout vegetation that reproduces according to its kind. In days four, five, and six, God created the sun and moon for day and night, put birds in the sky and sea creatures in the water, and made creatures for the land, culminating with the creation of humanity made after God's own image. By grouping the days this way, we see that God worked the first three days to *form* the earth and then days four, five, and six to *fill* the earth, thereby fixing, across the space of the creation week, that twofold issue of the earth being formless and empty.[3]

God's pattern of forming and filling the earth in the space of six days contains further details that show how God made the world functional and gave it order.[4] Moreover, this order serves to promote human life so that we might have communion with God. The first day recounts the creation of light, which differentiated day from night:

> And God said, "Let there be light," and there was light. And God saw that the light was good. And God separated the light from the darkness. God called the light Day, and the darkness he called Night. And there was evening and there was morning, the first day. (Genesis 1:3–5)

This newly introduced distinction between day and night crucially functions to mark the passage of time within the world, which is especially clear in the text's pattern of marking the close of each of God's creative acts by noting the end of a successive day.[5] So God's work on the first day ordered the dependable progression of time.

This pattern of day and night importantly ordered God's own work routine across the rest of the creation days. According to the progression of days, God would begin his work in the morning but cease in the evening, completing something within the workday then resting after the task. We must remember that when talking about God working and resting, we are speaking *metaphorically*. God does not need time to accomplish his will since he *could* bring it about instantly but could *not* tire and need rest. Still, Scripture depicts God as working throughout the day and ceasing to work at night.

Why is this order important? Because God patterned his routine that way, revealing it to us in Scripture, so that we would know that it is our proper order too.[6] The process of working each day and ceasing work at the end of the day is meant to teach us that humanity's natural pattern is the back and forth of work and rest. As John Calvin argues concerning the phrase "the first day,"

> Here the error of those is manifestly refuted, who maintain that the world was made in a moment. For it is too violent a cavil to contend that Moses

> distributes the work which God perfected at once into six days, for the mere purpose of conveying instruction. Let us rather conclude that God himself took the space of six days, for the purpose of accommodating his works to the capacity of men ... God applied the most suitable remedy when he distributed the creation of the world into successive portions, that he might fix our attention, and compel us, as if he had laid his hand upon us, to pause and to reflect.[7]

Although God is outside time, God created light to mark the passing of days within creation to remind us constantly that we are bound to time and its forward march. This order is meant to set a routine for us as we live in the world and live our lives before God. We too are meant to go about our work, engaging in useful, contributing tasks, yet also make sure to take time to cease our work.

In the western world, we have largely forgotten the patterns of working and resting, letting work and busyness overrun our lives. Many of us, myself included, have a hard battle to fight with workaholism. We think, possibly because the hamster wheel of the corporate ladder of whatever field where we have our vocation ingrains it in us, that if we keep pressing ahead by doing more activities and more projects, then we will finally get ahead and be successful. We have forgotten the God-ordained pattern of work *and rest*.

We should not think, however, that rest entails meaningless idleness. Many things we ought to do are breaks from our work but are rest in another sense. To follow God's pattern for our lives, we must cease from our work but not necessarily from beneficial things. For example, breaking from our work-related tasks to get on the floor to play with our children is still a fruitful contribution but is nonetheless a break from our commissioned work. As much as we are not meant to be lazy in avoiding work, we are also not meant to define our lives entirely by our work. The idea of a "work-life balance" is a fabrication of an entertainment-driven society, since work is in fact part of life.[8] Nevertheless, work is only *one* part of life that should not crowd out its other parts. Reorienting our focus to include other aspects of life is a critical way in which we maintain God's properly ordered design for us.

God's work in establishing the pattern of day and night to govern the routines of human life was not the end of God's work in authoring order. On the second day, God distinguished the waters that were above and below the expanse:

> And God said, "Let there be an expanse in the midst of the waters, and let it separate the waters from the waters." And God made the expanse and separated the waters that were under the expanse from the waters that were above the expanse. And it was so. And God called the expanse Heaven. And there was evening and there was morning, the second day. (Genesis 1:6–8)

The expanse and its surrounding waters have been understood differently by various Bible interpreters. The most convincing interpretation—following Calvin, Peter Van Mastricht, and several modern biblical scholars—is to see this expanse between the waters as the atmosphere between the clouds as the upper waters and the seas as the lower waters, which were not yet distinguished from the land. In day two, the earth was still plainly covered in deep waters, namely the seas, forming the lower waters (Genesis 1:2). Even the ancients knew that clouds were made of water, so this view does not read something foreign into the text in seeing them as the upper waters. After all Psalm, 148:4 summons "the waters from above the skies" (my translation) to praise God, indicating that these upper waters still remain part of our world today. This second day then describes the ordering of atmospheric processes with air and clouds, so that life forms that God would make would have an adequate habitat in which to live.[9]

We learn that God is hospitable. Many connect the idea of Christian hospitality specifically to our evangelistic efforts, as if being nice to others is a means to winning them to the community of faith. Genesis 1, however, teaches us that God set a place to welcome others before any need to win sinners to salvation existed. The call to hospitality is then a summons to imitate God in his creational disposition. There are many ways to be hospitable according to our own capacities. Not everyone has to host thirty people for lunch at your home after church every Sunday. Many will find other ways that play to their own abilities and resources better—the fellowship committee at my church is full of people who invaluably give their time to make our whole church more hospitable regardless of how they may or may not host people in their own homes. All the same, we all need to follow God's creational pattern of hospitality by working to make space for others in some way.

God's work of ordering the form of creation culminated in providing clearly defined places for his creatures to live. In day three, he made a clear distinction between the land and sea:

> And God said, "Let the waters under the heavens be gathered together into one place, and let the dry land appear." And it was so. God called the dry land Earth, and the waters that were gathered together he called Seas. And God saw that it was good. (Genesis 1:9–10)

This distinction between land and sea provided the order needed to support the differing kinds of creatures that God intended to make. In day three, God did one more work of ordering creation with greater functionality. In this work, he further formed the land by adding vegetation to it:

> And God said, "Let the earth sprout vegetation, plants yielding seed, and fruit trees bearing fruit in which is their seed, each according to its kind, on the earth." And it was so. The earth brought forth vegetation, plants yielding seed according to their own kinds, and trees bearing fruit in which is their seed, each according to its kind. And God saw that it was good. And there was evening and there was morning, the third day. (Genesis 1:11–13)

When God created plant life, he formed it to reproduce *according to its kind*. God's authorship of order is profoundly clear in making the plant life with the ability to make more plants according to their kind.

This order is significant to human life. Imagine if you planted an apple seed, but a chicken grew up out of the soil and began running around. My guess is that you would be very confused, and rightly so. Our lives would be much harder if apple seeds could just as easily produce rocks or chickens as trees. The very idea of apple orchards, vineyards, dairy farms, fish hatcheries, and so forth would have to be thrown away if there were not an ordered predictability to the reproductive processes of vegetation and animals. The world would be fully disordered, as the lack of standard expectations in reproduction would wipe out our ability to organize agriculture, society, and vocational training. Creation would be random chaos.

Because God is the God of peace rather than confusion, however, he authored the natural world with order (1 Corinthians 14:33a). If you plant an apple seed, you get an apple tree. God cared that we be able to engage reliably with creation so that we could take part in cultivating the natural order itself and participate in building societies as we subdued the earth for God's glory. This dependability does more than uphold our ability to lead organized lives, seeking after specific kinds of food and decorating our homes with particular types of houseplants. God built the universe with a stable structure and predictable processes on which sound scientific investigation depends. Reliable examination relies on the inherent stability seen in our doctrine of creation. The scientific method of proposing a hypothesis and repeatedly testing it for accuracy presumes that the same combination of materials or cause-and-effect relationships is stable and recurring. In this way, our doctrine of creation, wherein God wrote order rather than randomness into the universe, is a fundamental premise of our approaching the world, investigating it, and making conclusions concerning how it works. Creation's natural stability is necessary for our cultivating habits and our investigations of nature.

Although God's authorship of order is perhaps clearest in his work during the first, second, and third days as he *formed* the earth, nonetheless his acts of *filling* the earth in days four, five, and six also contain rich marks of his purpose for order. In day four, God made the sun, moon, and stars so that they would govern the day and night (Genesis 1:14–19). More specifically, he intended them to "be for signs and seasons, and for days and years." As God assigned these lights to direct the passing of time, he brought further order to the universe's structure. He could have made the world with an unpredictable pattern of light and dark, but he made it so that the earth's rotation around the sun according to set laws of physics would ensure order for the patterns of human life according to various time measurements. God fixed order into how we experience the passing of time and *filled* the skies with bodies to govern time to ensure that the routines of our life with him are predictable.

The fifth and sixth days similarly reveal God's purposes to make the world with order by recounting how God made all his creatures, like the plant life, to reproduce *according to their own kinds* (Genesis 1:20–31). Animal breeders make their living off the dependability of certain dogs reproducing that same kind of dog and the predictability of mating somewhat different dogs. It was of great comfort to me when my wife was pregnant to know that my son would be born looking something like me rather than covered in cat hair. God hardwired each species so that they provide individual examples of God's purposes for order in creation. As God made all things, his purposes demonstrate the order of the universe, thereby proclaiming that the God who authored it is indeed the God of order.

OUR PARTICIPATION

Far from being an incidental facet of the physical universe, God's work to author order into creation summons us to live in specific ways because we are God's image bearers, designed to reflect him. Specifically, God's *process* of forming and filling the world reveals something of what we should reflect as his image bearers. God's ongoing creative acts of forming and filling the earth to author it with order display the intentional way he used his creative power to set a model for us to follow. Notwithstanding the enduring debates about how long the creation days truly were, we should all admit that God *could have* instantly made the world in its completed form.[10] Even if you believe that these creation days were not each literally twenty-four hours long as the solar days we know now are, God nonetheless inspired Scripture to describe the creation events as taking time. Certainly, God has revealed his pattern of working so that we might learn how God calls us to imitate him in our patterns of life.

Two lessons about our summons to imitate God as his image bearers emerge from the ordered patterns of Genesis 1. First, this narrative teaches that God made us for the purpose of vocation. Even though creation was in some sense complete once God formed and filled the earth, in another sense he commissioned humanity to carry on bringing it to greater completion:

> And God blessed them. And God said to them, "Be fruitful and multiply and fill the earth and subdue it, and have dominion over the fish of the sea and over the birds of the heavens and over every living thing that moves on the earth." (Genesis 1:28)

Just as God had continually filled the world as he ordered it increasingly under his dominion, he assigned Adam and Eve to further those creative and ordering works by filling the earth and exercising dominion over it. Therefore, having a task in the world—something at which we work—is part of our responsibility to reflect God's goodness into creation as his image bearers.

The second lesson from this narrative about our vocation to imitate God's work of forming and filling the earth is that we should reflect *the way* that God worked. Most pointedly, we learn a lesson about patience. God's use of time to bring about what is good teaches us to be patient in bringing about what is good. God did not need to use time to complete creation but chose to spread his work across the days. God carefully did what he thought best for each day, then rested. God called various stages of the process "good," pausing to appreciate work apart from assessing its completion. God's pattern of work then teaches us to exercise patience.

In today's culture, we tend not to cherish the routine and process of work. Moreover, we think that working endless hours makes us good and faithful employees. Instead of appreciating *the process* of accomplishing work in proportion, we fill every hour with work. We prioritize quantity over quality. We take sinful pride in working overwhelming hours as if we are better or more valuable for breaking God's pattern of work, often relishing that we feel we can outwork our Maker.

The importance of patient processes is something we should strive to recover. By way of illustration, this reminds me of how, when I was in high school, I used to build models of fighter jets and muscle cars. If you rush through the process of building these models and assemble them entirely in one go, the final product is rubbish. At the most basic level, a rushed job often results in shoddy assembly, leaving the parts not sitting flush. Even more, if you paint the model when the glue is not dry, the acid in the glue will easily make the paint fail to dry, and it will run everywhere. You must put a few pieces together at a time, leaving it to set and dry, then paint it and leave it to dry again. Part of the accomplishment in building models is appreciating *the process*, not just the *product*. If we cannot apply that practice across our lives, we throw away our vocations and even time, racing through tasks without enjoying what is.

God's pattern of decidedly appreciating the process of work and rest defines our participation in his image. Modern people, including Christians, need to learn that working endless hours does not define our value but makes us rebels against God's order for work. Setting a healthy pattern for accomplishing what you should today and leaving for tomorrow all else that could be done can be very difficult and, admittedly, requires wisdom. Still,

Genesis calls us to imitate God, whose image we were designed to reflect, by doing exactly that. If we do not rest at the end of each day, then we are not properly reflecting God.[11] God's moral example requires that we learn to rest after a period of work. Patience is then a virtue entailed by following God's example. Genesis calls you to slow down and appreciate the process of work in proportion. Our participation in God's order of creation, at least partly, is that we need to learn more about the pattern of life as creatures who depend on the passing of days and years and to appreciate patiently enjoying the process of our callings.

GOD'S PROMISES

The summons for us as God's image bearers to reflect God in our patterned and ordered habits of work and rest shows how our callings to various paid jobs or unpaid vocations are part of God's good purposes for creation, as is learning patience to appreciate the ongoing, routine process of those tasks. So, as God's creatures, we should have a natural love for our work and for serving the Lord in the world. Nevertheless, as sinners, we quickly distort God's good purposes, so we need to qualify how we relate to these facets of creation in light of our need for rescue from sin's curse.

We briefly need to jump ahead of ourselves concerning God's "process" of creating the universe. As we will see when we think about Genesis 2's description of the garden of Eden, that dwelling place was the first temple on earth, which God built so that Adam could live and work in it as a place for special communion with the Lord. This centers human life within a religious context of living in a place of special communion with God. Given that the true God's temple—the tabernacle in the wilderness, the Jerusalem temple, and the church—is always connected to his covenant relationship with his people, this point all the more centers human life in covenant with God.[12]

Humanity's first role was covenantal since God commissioned Adam to fill the earth, namely by spreading the garden-temple across the globe—a big point but one developed in later chapters. Adam's first work was temple-building work, meaning also that Adam's job was to expand the place of fellowship with God. As Adam and Eve multiplied the human race as our first parents, their children would have all the space they needed to commune with God in the global garden-temple. Adam's job was not simply to build a bigger temple but to enlarge the place of God's special presence. His work focused on the purpose of facilitating communion with God. Nevertheless, the story of Adam carrying out this purpose did not go smoothly.

On the one hand, God properly ordered us to specific purposes. He built us to work properly and to function well so that we could fulfill the ends for which he designed us. Creation shows a progression of ordered purpose, culminating in the Sabbath, which God consecrated that we would use it to join him in worshipful rest—an idea we will explore at length in a later chapter. God, then, as his pinnacle act of the creation week, appointed that Sabbath of worshipful rest as our highest purpose. So the ultimate end to which God ordered creation is communion in worship between God and his people.

On the other hand, fallen people are *disordered* by sin. Christians rightly emphasize the guilt of sin as a violation of God's covenant law but sometimes understate how sin's effects are not limited to its penalty. Sin also corrupted our nature. Whereas creation reveals that God ordered us *by nature* to the supernatural end of everlasting life, sin disordered everything about us, like opening your car's circuitry, clipping wires, and reattaching them randomly.

The apostle Paul describes this dysfunctional effect of sin in Romans 1:18–32. He writes in verses 21–23:

> For although they knew God, they did not honor him as God or give thanks to him, but they became futile in their thinking, and their foolish hearts were darkened. Claiming to be wise, they became fools, and exchanged the glory of the immortal God for images resembling mortal man and birds and animals and creeping things.

This wrongful rewiring of our constitution means that our sin must be addressed in more fundamental ways than we may realize. Salvation deals not *only* with sin's penalty, as in justification, but also with sin's power, as in sanctification.

We often think that sanctification is about committing to do individual good things more often as if it is about growing in our toughness to say "yes" to what is good and "no" to what is bad. However, Westminster Shorter Catechism question 35 says, "Sanctification is the work of God's free grace, *whereby we are renewed in the whole man after the image of God*, and are enabled more and more to die unto sin, and live unto righteousness."[13] Sanctification does include a growing ability to do good and shun evil, as Titus 2:11–12 makes clear: "For the grace of God has appeared, bringing salvation for all people, training us to renounce ungodliness and worldly passions, and to live self-controlled, upright, and godly lives in the present age." Still, we cannot reduce sanctification to its effects in the deeds it enables us to do.

After all, as the Catechism says, sanctification is first the renewal of the whole person, producing a continual rewiring of our persons back to what God originally ordered us to be like. This rewiring—a reordering—means all those wires that we by our sin have attached in the wrong places must be cut and reattached in the right places. This rewiring so that we are properly ordered again to want, love, and desire what is good can be painful as those wires are clipped but brings the great reward of being truly human when we are again properly ordered.

So, just like we must learn patience in the daily affairs of life, we must also learn patience in our sanctification as individuals and as churches. God takes our lifetime to sever the wires in our hearts that power wickedness. Sanctification is more than working hard at resisting temptation. It rewires your heart so you not only resist disparaging others but prefer collegiality to personal prestige. It reorders your person so you not only resist pornography but desire only your spouse and respect humans made in God's image rather than *wanting* to fulfill lustful longings.

That heart-level rewiring takes a long time to bring about these changes in us as individuals but is where we need to focus our efforts. Temptation is not a moment *simply* to tough it out but an opportunity to see your circuitry rewired. Every time that you give in to that temptation, it makes it harder to divert the current next time. We get programmed to give in to sin, and keeping with our default programming only intensifies its hold on us. But every time you decide for faithfulness, it builds a stronger pathway and a stronger habit of holiness. We cannot flinch just because temptation feels harder but must be patient in pressing forward so that our hearts truly and deeply change.

The same point applies to us as we live out the Christian life in our churches. Christians easily get frustrated with their church for various reasons—some valid, some illegitimate. At the same time, a church is a bigger circuit board composed of smaller wrongly ordered circuits. We readily know what we wish our church would be like but must be patient, knowing that the imperfections or failures that can mark any church exist because we as individuals contribute by our sin. So, we learn to be patient with our church, praying hard for its holiness and working calmly to see it grow in depth and number over time.

Despite this ongoing war against our own sinfully disordered nature, God's promises are fully displayed in his commitment to reorder his people to holiness. In Romans 8:29, Paul writes that God has predestined his elect to be conformed to Christ. *God* reorders us through sanctification. *He* will conform us to Christ because the gospel entails that he who gave his Son for us—as he died to forgive our sins and rose for our justification—will with him graciously give us all things. Whereas we so often find ourselves working like a watch with hands turning the wrong way, God reorders us so that we function as he intended.

CONCLUSION

God reorders us primarily through the very thing toward which he originally ordered us: rest in worship on God's appointed day, the Lord's Day, through the ordinary means of grace. Our great privilege is to be ordered toward communion with our God, and even when that seems distant, it is our great privilege that God reorders us to that communion by meeting us despite our sin and speaking to us as he summons us into the communion of worshipful rest. The book of Genesis is thoroughly about our communion with God by both creation and redemption. He uses his Word, like the text of Genesis, to strengthen us in Christ that we might walk with him in fuller communion all the days of our lives.

QUESTIONS FOR FURTHER REFLECTION

1. How does God's creative work fulfill an effective design? Think of specific examples in the plant and animal kingdoms.
2. Since God can operate outside and apart from time, why did he choose to create light and darkness to

mark the passing of time? What does this teach us about patience?

3. As image bearers of our Creator, how do we reflect his work of forming and filling?
4. What does God's pattern of work and rest teach us of our own patterns within our vocations? How has sin distorted our understanding of this divine pattern? Finally, how does the Lord's Day regularly reorient us toward this proper pattern?

BEAUTIFUL COMMUNION

God the Bringer of Beauty

Vehicles become well known for very different reasons. On the one hand, we can think about functionality and resilience. On the other, there are handling and aesthetics. Advertisers market a Dodge Ram by focusing on features like how heavy a payload it can carry and its towing ability. This sort of vehicle will endure through heavy paces. It is tough and will get the job done. On the other hand, in a factory called the Atelier, named after an artist's studio, "craftspeople"—as the company calls them—assemble Bugatti sports cars by hand, aiming for incomparable performance and tailoring each vehicle to the specifications set by the person buying it. Even a fleeting glance impresses on one the difference between these vehicles. A Dodge Ram may be excellent at getting the job done. A Bugatti, however, is elegant. Craftmanship manifests itself in various ways through equally durable and functional vehicles. But a Bugatti will turn your head as it passes because it has not only performance but also beauty. In ways that the battering-ram appearance of a pickup truck never could, the gently sloping lines and scooped doorframes on these performance sports cars demonstrate how things that work can also be very beautiful.

God's glory has already been a prominent theme as we have meditated on Genesis so far. Concerning Genesis 1:1–2, we first saw how God's first act of creation put his magnificent transcendence on full display. In the previous chapter, our first thematic pass through the creation narrative showed how God built creation so that it would be properly ordered to his intended purposes, the highest being to facilitate communion between him and us as his image bearers. These basic points reaffirm this book's main idea that Genesis 1–2 summons believers to contemplate the riches of our communion with God.

This chapter builds on these truths by exploring how our communion with God is not just majestic and ordered but also beautiful. God made the earth not simply into a place that works, like a Dodge Ram, but into a place that is also beautiful, like a Bugatti. As we will see, God's work of making a beautiful creation has profound relevance for the way that we think about the world and live in it. As we meditate on the Lord himself, his works of beautifying creation teach us the main point that God is not a pragmatist but cares about what is true, good, *and beautiful.*

GOD'S GOODNESS

This second thematic pass through the creation narrative uses the lens of beauty rather than order. God did not forge a *simply* functional earth but made a wonderful earth. Keeping in mind our lessons about work from the previous chapter, we now learn that our work should be not just properly ordered but also enjoyable—as far as possible this side of the curse—and should contribute to the betterment, even the beautification, of the lives of people around us.

Again, God's working over the creation so that it is no longer formless and empty frames a crucial theme in the rest of the narrative.[1] This idea even appears in other parts of Scripture. The prophet declares in Isaiah 45:18:

> For thus says the LORD,
> who created the heavens
> (he is God!),
> who *formed* the earth and made it
> (he established it;
> he did not create it empty,
> he formed it to be inhabited!):

The Scripture identifies God by his creative activity, naming how creation was formed and not empty. Although Isaiah's prophecy might *seem* at first appearances contrary to what Moses wrote in Genesis, his point is simply that God's creation was not formless or void by the end of the creation process.[2] That little phrase "without form and void" may not have prompted extended reflection among many devoted readers of Scripture but is nonetheless very important, signaling the very concern that God addresses throughout the six creation days.[3] The key issue is that the Bible returns to the idea of God overcoming the creation's formless and empty state, even linking God's identity to this glorious work.

So, just as this "problem" of the earth's formless and empty condition shaped our first thematic pass through Genesis 1 concerning God authoring order in creation, so it again guides our second thematic consideration regarding God bringing beauty to creation. The problem facing God's work to beautify creation begins even before God began the first day of creation by creating light: "The earth was without form and void, and darkness was over the face of the deep. And the Spirit of God was hovering over the face of the waters" (Genesis 1:2). In this condition, no light illumined the world, and deep waters kept the earth from being properly habitable. The text does not explicitly say that waters covered every inch of the earth's surface, although that may have been the case, but indicates that these primeval waters excluded a clear distinction between land and sea. That role of the deep waters, over which the Spirit hovers like a bird, spotlights the two-pronged issue that the earth was formless and void or empty.

This time, the situation with the waters helps us think more specifically about how God changed the face of creation to bring it from chaotic to beautiful. Before God created light, these waters were not even visible. The distinction between light and darkness, day and night, enabled humanity—even if hypothetically since none of us yet existed—to participate in God's assessment of the world (Genesis 1:3–5). After all, the world was not simply dark; light did not yet exist. Without light, creatures could not render any verdict about the world's goodness or make use of it. We could not recognize the world's beauty.

Even more, the waters themselves indicate a chaotic scene. Regardless of what beauty the land may have had, we could not see it under the cover of the deeps. Even if the water did not cover every square inch of the earth's surface, at best the situation involved predominantly the dark and murky cover with sporadic craggy outbreaks—hardly a scenic landscape. In the Hebrews' mindset, water itself represented danger since they were not a seafaring people. In the Song of the Sea, which Israel sang after God rescued them from Egypt by splitting the Red Sea, Moses—who also wrote Genesis—recorded:

> In the greatness of your majesty you overthrow your
> adversaries;
> you send out your fury; it consumes them like stubble.

At the blast of your nostrils the waters piled up;
the floods stood up in a heap;
the deeps congealed in the heart of the sea.
(Exodus 15:7–8)

As the Israelites rejoiced about their redemption, they noted that God's weapon against their enemies was "the deeps," the same Hebrew word appearing in Genesis 1:2 (תְּהוֹם, *tehôm*). Far from calming, the deeps were a threatening force. Further, the creation deeps were covered in darkness, another ominous indicator. Proverbs uses this same Hebrew word for "darkness" (חֹשֶׁךְ, *ḥōshek*) to describe the wicked "who forsake the paths of uprightness to walk in the ways of *darkness*" (Proverbs 2:13).[4] This combination of words, therefore, marks a problematic rather than an idyllic state of the earth. The point becomes clearer if we simply remember that at another major juncture in Genesis, God judged the world by a humanity-destroying deluge of deep water (Genesis 6:9–8:18).

God's work to remold this original state then not only makes it functional for human life so that we can commune with him but also removes its threatening, ugly appearance to make it a beautiful and peaceful place for that communion. We might think of the difference between the introductory scenes for the homes of Count Dracula and Frodo Baggins. In Dracula movies, we typically first meet the vampire in his castle's entry hall, which is filled with long shadows, drafty coldness, and an ominous emptiness that together suggest the sense of fear we should have in this environment. By contrast, in The Lord of the Rings, Frodo's home in the Shire shines with earth-toned brightness, hospitable warmth, and a coziness created by a home full of personal and familial possessions. Although we are not supposed to judge books by their covers, appearances can make all the difference when it comes to setting up a welcoming and intimate environment for communion.

God's first act that addresses this need for an improved environment was the creation of light on day one. We too readily take this provision for granted because we assume both light's role as part of our everyday lives and that its inclusion in creation was an obvious necessity. Yet God's creation of light has much to say about God's own character, his majesty, and his concern for beauty.

The payoff from this point is to grow in our thankfulness for how giving God is and how considerate he is for his people. God goes over and above to provide what we need, what will help us, and what will bless us. The key issue in this application is that God himself did not need light to perceive everything that was present in that original formless, void, and dark condition, even if he added to it without making light. God did not require light, but we would if we were to see his creation. In that respect, is it not amazing that God made light for us? He wanted us to be able not only to function in the world but to perceive its beauty.

God was also richly good in what he made for us to see, from the picturesque panoramas of ocean fronts or mountain ranges down to the sheer number of colors he made. I recently moved to Michigan, which is famous for its colorful leaves during the autumnal season change. I have noticed a particular shade of red, hanging in leaves on trees outside my office window, that I have never seen before. I am amazed by how beautiful this yet-unseen-to-me shade of red is. God did not have to create that specific shade of red. Further, even though God has imbued creation with such colored richness, he still did not have to make the human eye full of rods and cones so that we could perceive those hues. But God is rich in his goodness. He is not stingy but abundant. God's goodness is seen in how he created beauty and equipped us to appreciate it.

After God addressed the problem of darkness, he turned to the issue of the deeps. First, he made the waters useful, again reminding us of his concern to author order into creation. Thus, on the second day, God made an "expanse" that separated upper and lower waters. Far from requiring fanciful inventions of the imagination, that "expanse" is simply the sky or atmospheric layer around the earth that still remains. As Psalm 19:1 sings, "The heavens declare the glory of God, and the sky above proclaims his handiwork." The word translated "sky" in Psalm 19:1 is the same Hebrew word that is translated "expanse" in Genesis 1:6 (רָקִיעַ, *raqiaʿ*). David's psalm, therefore, praises God for his glorious work in fashioning the sky, which still proclaims divine majesty, using the same terms as Moses's creation account, indicating that the sky that could impress David to worship was the same sky that God forged on the second day of creation. The sky God made at creation is the same sky whose wide-open panoramas of crisp, blue clearness move us to recognize creation's freshness and freedom. As Bible interpreters from John Calvin to modern scholars conclude, the sky divides the waters on earth from the clouds, which are floating water as even the ancients knew.[5]

God's final way of addressing the problem of the unbeautiful deeps occurred on day three as he distinguished the land and sea (Genesis 1:9–13). Now that the earth was no longer characterized by the primeval deeps, God covered the land with vegetation. The problem was truly solved as the waters, which are undoubtedly necessary for the world to function, had been not only subdued by being split apart by the lands but also beautified as they became a scene to view rather than an overwhelming danger. Oceanfront property is some of the most expensive real estate on the market globally because we value the scenic vistas of the tranquil surface of the waves that paper over the captivating mysteries of the deep. We would not have the privilege of these views had God not built the shorelines by separating the land and sea.

The point is certainly that God's works made the world beautiful. This sky, even with its functional system of clouds to water our ground, replenish our streams, and refresh our air, was undoubtedly far more beautiful with light bouncing across our atmosphere to create that blue canopy we know than as an unseeable dark mass. The clouds, even with their ordered functionality to provide for the plants and water systems, remain a delicate gift of provision, far more beautiful than the undifferentiated deeps as they bob across the skyline and invite our imagination to find various familiar shapes in their pillowed tufts. Even as God authored order, he did so in such a way as to bring beauty.

The second half of the creation week merely extended God's beautifying work. He had already begun to decorate the land with vegetation. Now with a formed earth, in days four, five, and six, he beautified each portion of his universal canvas by filling it with its needed inhabitants.[6] He painted the skies with countless stars, as well as the sun and moon, to remind his creatures even at night that the Lord has provided light for us. He filled the seas with fish, the skies with birds, and the land with animals and humans so that there would be creatures to appreciate every environment of this inhabitable world. There is then a reasoned pattern to the creation narrative that describes God bringing the world from something unusable and unattractive to something thriving and beautiful.

The creation events reveal that God increasingly fashioned a beautiful creation. Further, his own character as the one who appreciates beauty signals that his image bearers are also meant to recognize the beautiful. As God finished giving the world form, he declared three times that what he had done was good (Genesis 1:4, 10, 12). He repeated this declaration as he filled the earth, culminating in the "very good" pronounced upon his completed creation, specifically once humanity was formed (Genesis 1:18, 20, 25, 31). God wanted the world to be beautiful by being formed, by being filled, and by being good, all of which reflects his beauty.

GOD'S GENEROSITY

We easily miss the scope of God's beautifying work as he developed the world from the dark and murky state of the primeval waters to the flourishing system of nature with all its points of grandeur that we know today. The compressed narrative leaves out a lot of detail but nevertheless implies what we need to know. Obviously, the plants and trees created to reproduce "according to its kind" at least became all the different varieties of fruit-bearing vegetation that we know and eat today. The animals designed to reproduce "according to their kind" at least all procreated with enough variety to become every sort of species we now know (or do not know, for that matter). The point is that God built the world to demonstrate his generosity, clearly seen in how many different things he made, all of which benefit us and point us to the Lord's beauty.

God's goodness shines forth in how richly he ordered the world so that it does not simply work but is beautiful. We already considered how the vast array of colors built into the world mark God's generosity to his creatures so that we may enjoy what God made for us. The color spectrum has no end of variety, demonstrating God's genuinely infinite abundance in providing things for his creatures to appreciate. So, too, God's varied and beautiful creations mark his overflowing generosity.

Think for a moment about the presumed abundance of everyday things. For example, I remember once going with my dad to an orange grove in Florida to pick oranges. I was struck by a more extensive array of citrus varietals, manifesting a wider spectrum of flavors in oranges, than I ever knew existed. On reflection, we should be impressed by how God could have made oranges edible and nourishing but tasteless. Yet he made this fruit in such a way as to bestow vitamin C and be pleasing to the taste. Even then, God could have made nourishing and tasty oranges, but they did not have to be pleasing to the eye. Still, God made orange trees so that they would be dotted with blips of color that deepen the richness of our experience of the material world. The multifaceted layers of blessings, which we so often take entirely for granted, simply prove how overwhelmingly generous God is in the blessings that he built into creation because we cannot account for all those layers no matter how hard we try.

Part of our problem is that we live in an era in which we have constant access to all sorts of blessings, making it easy for us to overlook simple things that are truly mind-blowing gifts of God. Christian, Genesis 1 calls you to remember the richness of your God. When you go to the shop and walk through the produce aisle, being bombarded with colors and the prospect of endless flavors, you ought to stop and thank God for that generous beauty.

Further, God's generosity in creation not only calls us to appreciate God's goodness but also prompts us to consider again what it means to live as those made in God's image. God's image bearers are called to reflect God in his generosity. We who are made in God's image, and especially Christians who are renewed in God's image by Christ, need to be characterized more by giving than by collecting.

There are all sorts of more specific applications for this point. The obvious one that most have already considered, even if momentarily, is our wallets. Without dismissing the point that we should give as much as we are able to support our churches, perhaps we should think more deeply. Genesis does not prompt us to think as much about the matter of money as it does the issue of time. After all, these are the extraordinary *days* of creation.

God's creation work spread across the space of six days provides another rich lesson concerning what generosity entails respecting how we use our time. Augustine, the foremost theologian of the ancient church, argued that these days are figurative because God did not need six days to create since he could do it instantaneously:

> For this power of Divine Wisdom does not reach by stages or arrive by steps. It was just as easy, then, for God to create everything as it is for Wisdom to exercise this mighty power. For through Wisdom all things were made, and the motion we now see in creatures, measured by the lapse of time, as each one fulfills its proper function, comes to creatures from those causal reasons implanted in them, which God scattered as seeds at the moment of creation when *He spoke and they were made, He commanded and they were created*. Creation, therefore, did not take place slowly in order that a slow development might be implanted in those things that are slow by nature; nor were the ages established at plodding pace at which they now pass. Time brings about the development of these creatures according to the laws of their numbers, but there was no passage of time when they received these laws at creation.[7]

Though you may agree or disagree with Augustine about the days' length, he was surely right that God did not *need* that long. Still, Scripture describes God's work as six days.

The lesson for us is that God used his time, even when he did not need to spend it so, specifically for someone else's good. God was not the primary beneficiary of all his work to beautify creation. We are. God had all incomprehensible beauty to admire within his own being as the Father, Son, and Spirit eternally indwell and love one another.[8] God needed no further beauty to satisfy him. Creatures, however, cannot access God in his own essence and so must learn about the depth of his beauty from the things he creates. God voluntarily spent time improving the world not for his benefit but for ours. He donated those creation days so that we would be better positioned to know his beauty and be led to glorify him through the beautiful things he made.

Despite how God used his time and gladly gave it for someone else, how often do we *rush* through helping someone to get back to our own affairs? How often do we resent needing to *invest* our efforts to make something useful for someone else? God shows us that it is good and generous to work for someone else's benefit and to put your time out there for them. One of the best ways you can do this is by not being superficial in your interactions with people. Be generous with *yourself.* We live in an impersonal culture, but God is a personal God. Share your hardest struggles and deepest joys. Be honest and genuine. Listen well to one another. Be ready to share your real self in conversation. Do not respond superficially but take the deep dive into people's lives to relate to them. God's generosity prompts us to be more amazed at God's goodness in nature but also to be more generous ourselves.

GOD'S GIFTS

Our reflection on Genesis 1's teachings about God as the bringer of beauty needs to close by thinking about two types of gifts. Calvin helps us with the first by reminding us that the primary point of Genesis 1:29 is that God is the giver of all things we need, primarily food.[9] God invented a lush variety of foods and gave them all to us for nourishment. In ancient creation myths, the gods created humanity as workers to find and prepare food for them. Genesis, however, says our wonderful God made us and provides for us in all ways.[10] We should be thankful at all moments for our very sustenance but perhaps more pointedly grateful every time we eat. Praying for God's blessing on our meals is not an empty ritual but expresses dependence on our generous God and gratitude that he would use the means he created to provide the nourishment we need. Indeed, God is good to feed us, and our thankfulness for the food we receive should never run dry no matter how frequently we bow to render it to the Lord.

Think how abundantly and generously God has provided, even in food. In day three, God made a great many types of plants, giving them to humanity to eat. God could have made one plant for our food. He could have made plain porridge as our only source of nourishment but has made mangos, coconuts, asparagus, sweet potatoes, and so much more. Calvin's preaching on Genesis helps us see this point:

> When the earth was filled with all good things, when the animals, birds, and fish were created, and the crops and all that grows for food for men and beasts, all being good, God then created man. So, seeing that He began before our father Adam came into existence, let us call upon our God and take refuge in Him whenever some scarcity presses upon us, and let us not doubt that His hand is always open to do good for us and show that He is generous toward us.[11]

We can affirm with Calvin that the creation narrative emphasizes God's generosity.

Genesis 1's emphasis on vegetation for food does not necessarily prevent us from thinking more widely about God's goodness in the food we have (verse 29). That attention on the plants calls focus to eating fruit, foreshadowing Adam's coming test with the Tree of Knowledge.[12] For that reason so inherently tied to the significance of this narrative for sinners needing to understand how sin entered world, many interpreters in the Reformation tradition and before—including Calvin, Augustine, and Thomas Aquinas—argue that we were actually permitted to eat animals even before the fall.[13] This idea likely needs some explanation and application on its own before using it for our wider discussion.

We should emphatically distinguish the possibility of human death before the fall from the issue of animals dying apart from sin's entry into creation. The idea of *human* death before the fall is significantly problematic because of our doctrine that God made humanity in his image, a topic that the next chapter explores at more length. Humans bear God's image, entailing the likeness of the One who *is* life in himself and cannot die. Death does not befit the creatures who represent, at the creaturely level, the God who is life. Death was never natural to *human* existence.

On the other hand, animals are not God's image bearers. Even if this sort of thinking is new to us, given that many presume the lack of death before sin applied to all God's creatures, we should not conflate the necessary entailments of bearing God's image with God's purposes for his other creatures. Indeed, *our* sin as God's image bearers easily included death as its curse not only as the consequence of breaking God's law but also because it alienated us from the God who is life by making his image bearers more like those creatures who were not image bearers, seen precisely in how they could die. God did not make them to reflect his nature as the source of boundless, incorruptible life.

In this respect, the important considerations are biblical and ethical. We should not import foreign meaning into God's Word either for or against the topic of animal death before the fall but should account for the whole message of Scripture. Biblically, God claims credit for making the beasts of prey, who are skilled at killing their food. The book of Job is largely about Job learning to reckon with his suffering in light of God's sovereignty and care for his people. In the final section, God responds to Job with the reminder that he is not in the dock before his creatures but has acted wisely and sovereignly beyond our comprehension. As part of this response, God extols his work of making some animals well-designed for killing prey:[14]

> "Can you hunt the prey for the lion,
>   or satisfy the appetite of the young lions,
> when they crouch in their dens
>   or lie in wait in their thicket?" (Job 38:39–40)

God boasts that he provides prey for lions when they use their hunting skills as stealthy predators, implicitly extolling his work of crafting a vicious hunter of other animals. The lion, however, is not God's only well-designed hunter.

> "Is it by your understanding that the hawk soars
>   and spreads his wings toward the south?
> Is it at your command that the eagle mounts up
>   and makes his nest on high?
> On the rock he dwells and makes his home,
>   on the rocky crag and stronghold.
> From there he spies out the prey;
>   his eyes behold it from far away.
> His young ones suck up blood,
>   and where the slain are, there is he." (Job 39:26–30)

God also reminds Job of his wisdom in crafting birds of prey, which are able to hunt from long distances because of how God equipped them with eyes able to see far away. Throughout Job 41, God climaxes his commendation of his own ability to design hunters by describing the leviathan, which was possibly the animal that we call a crocodile. Among the various ways in which the wise God designed this most ferocious beast, God highlights:

> "I will not keep silence concerning his limbs,
>   or his mighty strength, or his goodly frame.
> Who can strip off his outer garment?
>   Who would come near him with a bridle?
> Who can open the doors of his face?
>   Around his teeth is terror.
> His back is made of rows of shields,
>   shut up closely as with a seal.
> One is so near to another
>   that no air can come between them.
> They are joined one to another;
>   they clasp each other and cannot be separated."
>   (Job 41:12–17)

God refuses to be silent, rather celebrating how he crafted leviathan. Among all leviathan's fierce features, its *teeth* and shielded back are noteworthy. God's commendation of this creature's terrible teeth marks how he designed it to eat its prey, and his commendation of its defensively armored skin shows how he knew it needed protection from other animals. So, in *Scripture*, God extols his design of fierce hunters among the animals.

God's celebration of these ferocious predators marks his purposes for them. Importantly, the descriptions of these animals take place within God's reply to Job, summarized under his question:

> "Where were you when I laid the foundation of the earth?
> Tell me, if you have understanding.
> Who determined its measurements—surely you know!
> Or who stretched the line upon it?" (Job 38:4–5)

As God reminds Job of his place before his Lord, he appeals not to the world's fallen condition but to his design in *creation*. In this respect, his commendation of some animals' ability to hunt is marked. It is hardly likely that God would commend aspects of fallen creation to extol his wisdom. It is all the more unthinkable that God designed his creatures, which he called good, with features that would help them fulfill their purpose only in the context of sin. Rather, God's purpose for some animals to hunt one another distinguished his purposes for animals from his purposes for humans, who were not designed for natural death but made liable to it only because of our sin.

God's *good* design of some animals as predators skilled at killing other animals not only distinguished humanity, as the image bearers of the God who is life, from the animals but also informed Adam's relationship with God at creation. In the garden, God's explicit threat of death and implicit promise of everlasting life for Adam (as chapter eight explores) would make little sense if humans naturally died before sin entered the world. Concerning God's curse of death as sin's consequence, however, this threat of possible human death almost required that Adam knew exactly what death meant, which animal death would have shown to him.

This line of thinking is not merely a speculative leap. In Scripture, God regularly curses sinners by making them *more like the beasts*. In Daniel 4:28–33, King Nebuchadnezzar boasts about his accomplishments in building Babylon for the glory of his own majesty, prompting God to curse him. God curses Nebuchadnezzar's pride by making him like the animals:

> While the words were still in the king's mouth, there fell a voice from heaven, "O King Nebuchadnezzar, to you it is spoken: The kingdom has departed from you, and you shall be driven from among men, and your dwelling shall be with the beasts of the field. And you shall be made to eat grass like an ox, and seven periods of time shall pass over you, until you know that the Most High rules the kingdom of men and gives it to whom he will." Immediately the word was fulfilled against Nebuchadnezzar. He was driven from among men and ate grass like an ox, and his body was wet with the dew of heaven till his hair grew as long as eagles' feathers, and his nails were like birds' claws. (Daniel 4:31–33)

Nebuchadnezzar himself, while describing his dream, summarizes this curse: "Let his mind be changed from a man's, and let a beast's mind be given to him; and let seven periods of time pass over him" (Daniel 4:16). Daniel also threatened the same fate for Belshazzar if he continued in his father's same pride (5:21–22). Outside Daniel, Peter and Jude both describe sinners with blind minds as being made like the unreasoning beasts (2 Peter 2:12; Jude 10). Psalm 49 reflects on how to live in light of our inevitable death, clearly having an eye to how death is not the ideal end to human life. Still, twice the psalmist remarks that "Man in his pomp" meets death by becoming "like the beasts of the field that perish" (Psalm 49:12, 20). Although human death *problematically* ends our life, it makes us like the animals for whom death seems more acceptable. After all, no one would object had Adam killed the serpent who tempted him and Eve in the garden, so preventing sin altogether.

When God threatened Adam with death, then, this curse made sense to Adam because he knew what animal death was. Implicit in this curse was that death would contravene human dignity by making us more like the animals who did not bear God's image and so were susceptible to death by nature. Death is especially unfit for humanity because we are meant to reflect the God who is unending life, marking us as distinct from the animals, who differed greatly from us in the degree of their glory and fitness for everlasting life (Psalm 8:5–8; Hebrews 2:5–9).

Far from an arcane matter about creation, the animals' susceptibility to death before the fall marks the dignity of human beings as those unique and special creatures for whom death is utterly foreign to God's design for us. We might highlight this special dignity's value, separating us from the animals in our design for unending life, for its significance in helping us refute the practice of abortion. Christian theology has long recognized that life begins at conception, meaning that the termination of a human embryo is an act of killing a child.[15] Recent shifts in western culture and legislation have required us to defend this ethical truth more vigorously than ever.

Humanity's distinct dignity as God's image bearers, alone among God's creatures in having unending life intended for them, underscores the importance and cogency of the pro-life position. The incorrect supposition that a fetus is simply a clump of cells fails because it ignores how, uniquely among all his creatures, God wrote immortality into his image bearers' DNA. The human child, even from conception, is an ensouled being made for glory, honor, and eschatological destiny, sharply distinguishing him or her from all the other animals even by creation. We need not hold to strict vegetarianism nor need we deny that we will eat meat at the Lamb's eschatological wedding feast to uphold a consistent pro-life position about human birth. We mark humanity's unique place among all God's creatures as distinctly designed for unending life, making it distinctly degenerate to terminate a human life unjustly, even when that person has not yet been born. God's purpose for humanity to be unique among his creatures in the way that we should have possessed life, apart from sin, underscores how the murder of human life is an extravagant crime, exceptionally poised against nature and God's design for it holistically.

To help us make sure we line up this view with Scripture's details, we should account for how this idea hangs together with the events of Genesis 9:1–4. After Noah and his family emerged from the ark and God covenanted with Noah about upholding the created order (Gen. 8:18–22), God instructed Noah about life after the flood. He first commanded Noah to take up the task to be fruitful and multiply throughout the earth. Then, he said to Noah:

> The fear of you and the dread of you shall be upon every beast of the earth and upon every bird of the heavens, upon everything that creeps on the ground and all the fish of the sea. Into your hand they are delivered. Every moving thing that lives shall be food for you. And as I gave you the green plants, I give you everything. But you shall not eat flesh with its life, that is, its blood.

The question is, was God's instruction here the first time that humans were permitted to kill and eat animals? Even if we were not allowed to eat animals before this moment, animals may still have been allowed to eat one another, which can help us maintain our earlier considerations about God designing the predators with their skills and how beasts differ from humanity. The question about our relation to animals as food still needs an answer.

The emphasis in Genesis 9:2–4 is likely on the provision of *every* animal for food. In Genesis 7:2–4, God commanded Noah to take a male and female pair of *every* animal onto the ark but seven male and female pairs of all the clean animals. Before the flood, therefore, Noah worked with an understanding of the distinction between clean and unclean animals. Those clean animals would be needed for sacrifices at least after Noah left the ark.[16] As John Calvin pointed out, even prior to Genesis 9, we were likely meant to eat the meat of sacrificed animals, which would have been a meal in recognition of fellowship based on an accepted sacrifice.[17] Abel was earlier farming livestock precisely to have them for sacrifices and likely for meals as well since the sacrifices were only the firstborn portion of the herd and only the fat portions of the lamb offered (Gen. 4:2–4).

These considerations suggest than, in Genesis 9:1–4, God was likely removing the clean-unclean distinction from his provision for humanity to eat the animals. Noah received permission to eat, notably, "everything *that creeps on the ground*."[18] Later under the Mosaic covenant when the distinction of which animals were clean or unclean for food was a matter of grave importance for separating Israel as God's covenant people from the surrounding nations, God was emphatic about not eating this very sort of animal. In Leviticus 11:41–44, God restricted the permissibility of eating the swarming sorts of ground-dwelling animals, culminating in the prohibition: "Because I am the LORD your God, consecrate yourselves and be holy because I am holy. Therefore, you shall not make yourselves unclean with all the swarming creatures *that creep upon the ground*." (my translation)[19] These creatures that creep upon the ground were in particular focus as detestable under the clean-unclean distinction when it was in force to limit which animals God's people may eat. For Noah, however, God removed this ceremonial distinction, thereby widening the scope of which animals were permissible for food. The provision in Genesis 9:3 was then not about giving permission to eat animals for the first time ever but about removing the clean-unclean distinction from which animals we were allowed to eat for the purposes fitting a particular period in redemptive history.[20] God gave Noah *every* animal for food.

Despite our brief detour about God's purpose for animals in creation, our main point concerns God's goodness to his people in providing food for us, allowing *us* by creation even to eat animals. God's rich provision in his gift of meat for our sustenance underscores not only his basic care for us but also his abundant generosity because now we can think, even from Genesis 1, about how many animals God made and how tasty many are. Friends, if you were ever to visit Gulf Shores, Alabama, and eat a fried shrimp po'boy from one of the outstanding seafood restaurants there, you would indeed *know* by experience that God is good. We are supposed to enjoy God's creation. God made us from the dust of the earth, which fundamentally ties us to creation, which God said is good. We cannot escape being bound to the created earth. Heaven is not finally disembodied life, but as the Apostles' Creed summarizes 1 Corinthians 15, Christians have always confessed that we "believe in the resurrection of the body." God well-made us as part of this physical world, dependent on it for so many things like food, and that is beautiful.

The second type of gift that Genesis 1's teaching on God as the bringer of beauty highlights is all the greater than God's natural provision in food and other physical needs because it is his supernatural provision in restoring by Christ even more blessings than we lost in Adam. Even before sin is introduced into the biblical narrative, the creation account already sets the stage to display the Savior as God's greatest gift to us. The story goes that creation was characterized by unformed waters, leading the way for Adam to come through those creation waters, enter the garden, be tested, but fail. Much the same, as Moses's Song of the Sea already foreshadowed, Israel came through the waters of the Red Sea, went into the Promised Land, and proved faithless to the law. But as the true Israel, Jesus came through the waters of the Jordan at his baptism, went into the wilderness to be tested, and proved fully faithful (Matthew 3:13–4:11). Whereas Adam and Israel received the law personally *and then* were tested for themselves, Jesus was tested and succeeded for us, *only then* explaining our responsibilities of godliness in the Sermon on the Mount (Matthew 5:1–7:29). The law comes to the Christian in our life with God *only after* Jesus has fulfilled it and passed our test for us.

CONCLUSION

God's work of bringing beauty to creation by drawing Adam through the first waters points to how God restores beauty in us through the work of Christ as the waters of baptism poured on us symbolize how Christ washes us clean from sin, helping us walk in new faithfulness. We ought to believe in the God who was good in authoring order in creation but must also trust Jesus Christ as our Savior, the author, perfecter, *and beautifier* of our faith. Our God is a beautiful God. He has given us a functional but beautiful world to enjoy. Even more, our beautiful God has given us a beautiful Savior and offers the certain promise of everlasting life to all who would take hold of Christ by faith.

God's work of crafting beauty in the world has an immediate practical ramification. Too many people walk around even the most glorious locations on earth with their faces toward the ground, locked on some digital screen. We would be astounded more often if we lifted our heads from our mind-mushing social media accounts and looked toward the horizon. The skies are brighter, the cityscapes more striking, and the world around us more engrossing than we often realize. Commit yourself to leaving your phone in your pocket when you go out into the world. Lift your eyes and see what God has crafted.

QUESTIONS FOR FURTHER REFLECTION

1. How does God's act of creation transform the chaotic into beautiful?
2. How does God's beautiful creation testify to his abundant generosity? What does this teach us as image bearers?
3. How does God's generous work of provision at creation foreshadow his greatest gift?

MADE FOR COMMUNION

Reflecting God's Image

When you look in the mirror, you expect to see something that resembles your face. You know essentially what you look like, so you anticipate that your reflection should share your appearance. You want to see an image with eyes, ears, and nose arranged and shaped so that your distinct appearance gazes back at you in the mirror. Mirrors are in fact designed to provide you with an accurate image of yourself.

Reflections are part of God's properly ordered creation. Mirrors help us keep track of how our appearance truly looks and help us improve it. They are meant to provide a clear and accurate representation of your condition. If you looked in the mirror and saw a green elephant rather than a person with your characteristics, you would know that something was wrong with the image. Given that it is roughly impossible for a human to acquire the appearance of a green elephant, you would know that this mirror is somehow defective. The device that was supposed to be ordered to properly reflecting your image has become disordered from its purpose.

The Bible's teaching that God made humanity in his image is incredibly important because it focuses our attention on what God ordered us to do in our properly functioning roles. God designed us as his *image bearers* to reflect his character. We were meant to resemble God at the creaturely level, acting as his representatives in creation. This divine representation was meant to crown creation as properly ordered toward God's glory by installing a creature in the world that most directly manifested God's goodness but was also designed for the closest communion with him. In this respect, God declared that creation was very good once he created us according to his likeness (Genesis 1:31). A significant aspect of that "very good" was that he was properly represented in the world.

Despite God's very good work of fashioning his properly ordered image bearer to represent him in creation, by our sin we have come to distort God's reflection. Whereas initially we were very good, now no one is righteous and no one seeks for good. We are that mirror that shows a green elephant rather than a pristine reflection. Where we once carried God's goodness into the world by exercising righteous dominion within creation, now we reflect a bent and crooked version of that divine character.

God's work to create humanity as his image bearers culminates the creation week by forging the capstone of his entire endeavor in each of the respects on which we have reflected together. God inspired Genesis 1–2 to focus on his works so that this text would be a means of grace to facilitate *our* communion with him. Throughout this account, then, God progressively works over the unformed and unfilled creation to author greater order into it and bring it to brighter beauty. God's plan for a both properly ordered and supremely beautiful creation has its pinnacle in humanity.

By crowning the creation week with the creature made in his image, God brought the whole world into its most refined orderly state. He had progressively polished creation's functionality so that it worked according to good principles to support life. When God created man in his image, he brought this work to a climax in two ways. First, by providing creation with a creature fit for a true relationship with him, God has pointedly ordered creation for its ultimate purpose, namely, to glorify him. Stamped with God's image and called into communion with him, humanity provides a point of relational contact wherein God has a creature who can consciously interact with him to know his love and appreciate his glory.[1] In humanity, God then properly ordered creation to himself for a relationship. Second, God brought creation to its highest ordered state by creating humanity in that he appointed man to have dominion over creation (Genesis 1:28), thus providing a royal creature who would maintain and develop the ordered condition that God had created.[2]

God's creation of humanity crowned his work to make creation beautiful as well, also in two ways. Importantly, these ways of culminating beauty are both oriented Godward rather than merely focused on our existence, as if we could consider ourselves apart from our inherent relationship with God. First, God finished his work of making creation beautiful by making us because we are the creatures who can truly appreciate the beauty of creation. We top God's beautifying work because he made us in such a way that we can join him in recognizing what is good and beautiful. As God rendered the verdict that what he saw was good, so we were meant to imitate him in admiring what is good. Second, our reflections will primarily focus on how God put a capstone on creation's beauty by making humanity because we represent God within creation. As the creatures stamped with God's own character, we make creation beautiful by reflecting God himself into it. We have disordered our purpose in this respect through our sin, making this function harder to achieve. Yet God has not let his purposes to make creation beautiful by having a creature who represents him and ingrains his character into the world be spoiled. This chapter explores the main point that our purpose as God's image is to reflect our Creator's goodness, which now we can do only because of Christ's work.

DESCRIBING GOD'S IMAGE

With the background of God as the author of order and bringer of beauty in place, as we turn to reflect more specifically on our place within God's creation, we need to outline *how* we as God's image bearers are properly ordered toward reflecting God's goodness. Even the way that God created us inherently marks us for a relationship with him. Among all the creatures, we are uniquely connected to God because we alone carry his image in our very nature. We are naturally oriented in the way that we were made toward a relationship with God but have tarnished ourselves by sin so that relationship is broken.

Throughout the creation week, the repeated refrain of "God said, 'Let there be ... ' And it was so" displays God's power in making things that truly work unto the end to which he appointed them. This refrain marks God's commands that bring aspects of creation into existence but also reveals how God's speech produced exactly what he commanded, resulting in each thing operating toward its designated role. The light distinguishes day and night, the sky truly separates earth and clouds, land and sea are distinct, and sun and moon do govern the day and night. God's word proves effective and powerful in each instance.

The second half of that refrain, "and it was so," always makes me think of Captain Picard on *Star Trek: The Next Generation.*

Picard would often end his commands with "make it so," meaning there was nothing more to say—the instruction just needed to be done. The phrase's significance becomes forcefully clear in one instance. In the episode "Datalore," an imposter posed as one of the key officers, the android Data, on the Enterprise's bridge. The imposter outlined a solution to the troubling scenario confronting the Enterprise. When Picard responded, "Make it so," the imposter replied, "Sir?" So, Picard rejoined, "Do it." The uncertain reaction helped reveal that he was an imposter, but Picard's reassertion of the "make it so" directive shows the fiat nature of the command. When the captain speaks an order to be so, it must be done.

All the more, when God speaks, creation must make it so. The universe has no place to talk back to God, to question his orders, or to second-guess his instructions but room only to respond positively by doing what God commanded. God spoke light, sun, and moon into existence, and they still govern day and night as he intended. God spoke land and sea into existence, and they still define the habitats of land and sea creatures as he intended. God's word is powerful enough to bring about everything he decrees.

In that respect, God also spoke humanity into existence, appointing them to the role of bearing his image. Now, there has been a long debate about what God's image means. After all, God has no body or parts, so it cannot refer to our arms, legs, and faces. Theologians have often wanted to find something distinct about human nature that makes us God's image. Some suggest that the fact that we have souls makes us God's image. Others have said that our ability to reason, which sets us apart mentally from all the animals, makes us God's image. Although our souls and minds make us fit to be the creatures in communion with God, these features of our constitution are not determinative of our role to bear God's image apart from his commands. Just like we primarily see the sun and moon's main purpose not in the cosmic orbs themselves but in their role in aiding earthly life, so too we need to locate God's image in the role and relationship that God gave us at creation.

Centering our understanding of what it means for us to bear God's image *on the role and relationship God gave us* focuses our attention on our function of representing God within creation.. The creation account itself highlights God's command to us in connection to our place in creation:

> So God created man in his own image,
> in the image of God he created him;
> male and female he created them.
>
> And God blessed them. And God said to them, "Be fruitful and multiply and fill the earth and subdue it, and have dominion over the fish of the sea and over the birds of the heavens and over every living thing that moves on the earth." (Genesis 1:27–28)

After stating the fact that God created us in his image, the narrative immediately highlights God's address to our first parents that we would fill the earth, subdue it, and have dominion over the other creatures. Notably, God's command to us as his image bearers reflects the very things God himself had been doing: forming a chaotic earth into greater order and filling it with beautiful things. So, as with the other features of creation that found their function in God's command, we likewise discover our function as God's image in how God addresses us.

This relational understanding of our role as God's image has further support in the New Testament's reflections on the topic. Clearly, the New Testament writings differ from the creation accounts because they describe redemption rather than creation.

This difference shifts perspective from how God originally made us to how God remakes us in salvation. Still, the apostle Paul connects our renewal after God's image to two aspects of our role in creation. In two places, he describes the nature of putting on the new man, which he specifies is connected to our original place in bearing God's image and likeness. In Colossians 3:10, he writes that Christians are those who "have put on the new self which is being renewed in knowledge after the image of its creator." In Ephesians 4:24, he similarly argues that Christians must "put on the new self created after the likeness of God in true righteousness and holiness." For Paul, knowledge, righteousness, and holiness stand out as marks of our image-bearing role.

We should, therefore, understand our privilege of bearing God's image in connection to God's commission upon our lives, the vocation he intended for us within creation. Westminster Shorter Catechism question 10 brings together Colossians 3:10, Ephesians 4:24, and Genesis 1:28, summarizing how "God created man, male and female, after His own image, in knowledge, righteousness, and holiness, with dominion over the creatures."[3] That digest of scriptural points about the divine image highlights the *function* of knowing truth, being righteous, demonstrating holiness, and ruling creation as God's representatives as the tasks that constitute faithfully being God's image. As God has properly ordered everything in the universe to fulfill its appointed end, we now see more specifically that God properly ordered humanity to reflect and represent him on the creaturely level. Although sinners cannot even begin to honor this task unless they are born of the Spirit (John 3:5-7), by creation we were made good and upright.

We properly represent God in whose image we are crafted when we manifest his truthfulness in our knowledge, his perfection in our righteousness, his goodness in our holiness, and his sovereignty in our limited but responsibly executed dominion.

Michael Horton explains: "We could say that human beings are those who reflect God's image not chiefly in *what they are essentially* but *in how they reply ethically*. Though they are determined *as* human persons by the mere fact of their creation as God's image, their *realization of the purpose* of their personhood depends on whether they correspond to God's intentions."[4] Being God's image highlights our commission to reflect God's character. God spoke us into being as his representatives, and it happened, but—unlike all the other facets of creation—we made a problem. God said, "Let us make man in our image," and it was so. Then the image said, "I'd actually rather have that other fruit than keep reflecting your righteousness." Whereas sun and moon, sky and earth, land and sea still do exactly what God commissioned them to do, humanity has discarded our commission in favor of our own desires.[5] We describe God's image by emphasizing the role God gave us to represent him, which leads us to consider our present fallen state in relation to bearing God's image.

DEFILING GOD'S IMAGE

An image is supposed to do something. Every image captures something's appearance but also does much more. A mirror helps monitor our appearance, a photograph preserves a memory, a poster motivates specific values. Images capture appearance, but they also perform a function. The same is true for us as God's image in that we are meant to represent our Maker on the creaturely plane. That function means that godliness is about more than *simply* keeping God's commands as individual deeds.

We might better see the deeper principle of reflecting God by thinking about an illustration from family life. Parents often encounter the difficulty of answering the repeated question "Why?" when instructing their kids. Understandably, it is easy enough to say "Because I said so" as the simple final appeal to raw authority. There may indeed be substantial, natural reasons for whatever a parent is telling her child to do, but parental authority is also an important factor. Perhaps, however, sometimes the appeal to raw parental authority without the deeper reasons might suggest those reasons are not there.

The trouble is that, at least recently, even Christians think that God is like a parent who has lots of commands but no reasons for them. We imagine that our obedience is *simply* keeping a list of things that God has said to do *as activities* rather than as holistic descriptions of what we should be like. As Geerhardus Vos said in a sermon delivered at Princeton Seminary, "'To be righteous' acquires the restricted meaning of being law-like, instead of God-like. Sin also loses its absolute character of disharmony with the divine nature."[6] Thus, Christians in the modern era have focused on *command* rather than *character*.

When Christians come to think this way, the unbelieving world becomes frustrated with us because the only answer that we have given to support our ethical positions is "the Bible says so." We seem dependent on that final appeal to raw authority but disconnected from our purpose. Although we are surely right in pointing to Scripture's instruction, we shortchange ourselves and others if we stop at the raw appeal to its authority when Scripture itself supports further answers. The Bible often focuses on *character* and *good as good*, which should shape human life as those made in God's image.

When reflecting upon God as the author of order, we used the illustration of a watch and how it needs certain features to work properly according to what it was designed to do. A watch needs a face, a dial, and hands but also needs to perform its role properly by having hands turn the right way and keeping proper time. If the hands turn the wrong way or the inner cogs cannot track time well, then this watch that has all the right features is really less than a watch. Even with all the right features in place, a watch can fall short of its purpose if it does not function correctly.

Regarding our role as God's image bearers, we can have those features of a soul and a rational mind that are needed to be God's image but still function inadequately in our purpose if our moral circuitry is wrongly wired. Since humanity is God's image, to be wrongly wired to love godless things means that we are not functioning in a truly human way. Even to work even internally against our purpose to represent God is to short-circuit what we were made to do. We have forgotten our purpose.

In pastoral ministry, I rely on my cell phone for a lot of things, especially being in touch with people from my church. I cannot imagine how disruptive it would be if every time I tried to send a text message to the other elders from our congregation, the message went to a random number rather than to the one I tried to message. Even though my message is still going out, phones are supposed to contact the people you have named. If your phone acted this way, you would be pretty quickly demanding a new device. Yours would not be working like a phone is supposed to work.

The point is that our sin makes us function in our capacity of God's image bearers like a phone dialing and messaging all the wrong people. That sort of phone is not acting truly like a phone. Since we are made to reflect God's image, sinners are not truly acting like humans. Even if we are still capable of performing functions, they are directed to the wrong ends, making our whole purpose off kilter.

This emphasis on purpose puts our focus concerning obedience not *simply* on carrying out God's commands but on having the proper character. We must rightly consider *both* God's authority over us, expressed in his commands, and his purposes for us that undergird those commands. Specifically, God's moral law has deeper foundations in God's own nature. God instructs us with particular moral laws because those laws describe God's own character. God is truth, so we should not lie but love truth. God is life, so we should not murder but love life. God is faithful to his bride, so we should avoid sexual immorality and adultery. The laws that we are to follow in our deeds are also descriptions of the Law-Giver's character.

This link between God's commands and God's character means we cannot be satisfied with merely keeping a list of doing right things. We must be concerned about our *virtue*, or the shape of our character. A virtue is a practiced habit and disposition. It is like a muscle to be strengthened. Just like you strengthen your bicep by flexing your arm with weight attached, so you strengthen your patience muscle by using patience in situations that require it. Our ability to act in godly ways improves as our character deepens in godliness.[7]

So, the more that by grace we develop and strengthen our disposition—our reflex or impulse—toward godliness, the more in tune we are with what it means to be truly human. If we visit our physician, we know that there is a problem if the doctor hits our knee with that little reflex-testing hammer but our leg does not move at all. A properly functioning person has a reflex in his or her legs. So too, the reflex in our soul should properly be toward godliness. When we encounter any situation in the world, our instant response ought to be to reflect the goodness of God. If our reflex is to anything else, then there is a problem, and we are not working in truly human fashion.

Sin disrupts our ability to have this reflex. As God assessed his works of creation, he repeatedly rendered verdicts about what is good. Part of our function as God's image is that we were created to imitate God by rightly assessing what is good and rendering true verdicts about it. Yet when the serpent came into the garden and tempted Adam and Eve concerning the tree of the knowledge of good and evil, they rendered the wrong verdict, not recognizing the serpent's wickedness as evil nor God's command as good (Genesis 2:9; 3:1–7). In the wake of that first sin, we have continued to follow suit, constantly believing lies that what is wicked is good and rejecting that which truly is good. This principle displays how sin rewired human nature from its created, righteous condition so that fallen humanity is sinful not just in specific deeds but in our hearts and at the character level.

Christians typically struggle with sin the most in this regard. Believers are usually good at being outwardly kind to others but deeply struggle not to be angry. I may be able to congratulate my successful friends outwardly but inwardly am full of envy and resentment. When we find ourselves wrestling in this way, we must ask ourselves why our hearts would be in such turmoil over these issues. The answer is usually that we have put our focus on representing ourselves and our interests rather than on representing God. In that case, even though we are supposed to be the mirror reflecting God's goodness, we depict that ugly green elephant to our neighbors. We defile God's image not only by refusing to do the things God commands but more so by refusing to be the sort of person he made us to be.

DEPICTING GOD'S IMAGE

Our commission as God's image to reflect God, as well as our failure to do so, leaves us in a precarious position. The watch that turns backward is destined to be discarded, and the mirror that reflects the green elephant is bound to be broken. How are we to think of our situation now as those whose purpose is to be oriented toward God yet have rebelled?

Since we have sinned against our God and fail to meet our purpose of reflecting his perfect goodness into creation, we are doomed for destruction. Every breath that does not align with perfectly reflecting God collects further torment as we peer down the barrel of eternity. We are all accountable to God for our sin because as Romans 2:14 says, at times even "Gentiles, who do not have the law, by nature do what the law requires." That leaves us without excuse or hope—unless we can find rescue.

We find all the hope we need in the Lord Jesus Christ. In terms of the need to reflect God's character perfectly, Hebrews 1:3 says that the Son is "the radiance of the glory of God and *the exact imprint* of his nature." Christ is the original, ultimate, and unsurpassable image of God, as he perfectly reflects God's every perfection, and does so eternally. As the divine Son, naturally sharing the divine essence, Christ can only manifest God in his absolute purity. Still, this Son who perfectly manifested divine radiance took the form of a servant because we needed someone in our nature to succeed at fulfilling *for us* all righteousness required of the divine image.

Whereas we are distorted mirrors marring God's image and therefore fit for destruction, the beautiful Son of God, who perfectly radiates divine majesty, sacrificed himself so that even as his glory was temporarily hidden on the cross he might rescue us from everlasting ruin. When we should be discarded as broken representations, Christ paid for our failures and remakes us in his likeness so that being predestined to be conformed to his *image*, our creation purpose might be restored. Being in Christ blesses us with the Holy Spirit to renew us: "Therefore, if anyone is in Christ, he is a new creation. The old has passed away; behold, the new has come" (2 Corinthians 5:17). God's work of regeneration, whereby he brings a dead and sinful heart to life, continually works out in our lives so that more and more we can reflect his holy character.

As we are restored to God's image in Christ, we now live with a tension and a responsibility. You see, that purpose to reflect God in knowledge, righteousness, and holiness means that God's law is stamped on our hearts and embedded in our nature. We cannot escape the news of the law since that standard of righteousness rings in our hearts as though we live inside a cathedral bell. We cannot outrun the law or how the law is hardwired into the fabric of our being.

For that reason, Christians struggle with the tension of the gospel: the law is *in us*, but the gospel must be delivered *to us*. We so badly want a way to appeal to our obedience for consolation because we are good at speaking the law to ourselves. All the while, we know that we have shattered God's law, leaving our obedience nothing more than a badly distorted reflection of what we were supposed to be. The tension resolves in learning to accept what is *delivered to us* in the news of Christ. That is why we need to *hear* the gospel. The law written on our hearts condemns us since we are so far from fulfilling its call. We need to hear the Word that God has written on the cross instead. We do not have to earn our place with God because Christ has earned it for us.

That gospel resolution to the tension of the gospel leaves us with a twofold responsibility both to listen to the gospel and to speak the gospel, both helping us know how we depict God's image. We too often fear that our Christian friends tire of the gospel message. But those who know their sin need to hear this news constantly just like you. We are all tired and frightened under the law. So, we give ourselves to listen and speak of Christ. We listen because we depict God's image now as we receive it from Christ, renewed after *his* likeness, "predestined to be conformed to the image of his Son," so that Christ might have all the glory as our older brother who works in us by the Spirit to help us walk faithfully as his renewed siblings (Romans 8:29). We speak because we depict God's image, at last following his pattern of rightly rendering verdict about what is good, recognizing what is preeminently good in the Lord Jesus Christ. Thus, we should declare his goodness. We *listen* because Christ speaks as the true image of God, who forged our pathway to everlasting life. We *speak* because we all too easily forget the way to everlasting life and need each other to point the way back to the free mercy of the gospel.

CONCLUSION

Our status as God's image bearers places a special dignity on the human race. God designed us as the particular creatures made to know him in a deep and spiritual sense. One way we were meant to fulfill our role as the divine image bearers was to reflect God's goodness into the world around us by demonstrating his own character in ours. Although we have distorted that commission, God has restored us to our special place as the creatures representing him through the work of Christ Jesus. Crucially, however, our place to reflect and commune with God is always creaturely, meaning that we must know God and relate to him by creaturely means. As the principles of our communion with God have already come to the fore through our explorations of Genesis 1–2, our next reflections consider the means by which God facilitated our relationship with him.

QUESTIONS FOR FURTHER REFLECTION

1. What does it mean to be made in the image of God?

2. God properly ordered humanity to reflect and represent him on the creaturely level. How do we properly fulfill this mandate?

3. Because of sin, how do we defile God's image?

4. What is the tension of the gospel? What is the twofold responsibility of the gospel's resolution to this tension?

A TIME FOR COMMUNION

The Sabbath

Music grips people deeply. It is common to find people debating the merits of their preferred genre. People who agree on the best genre may even end up disputing about the best artist within that genre. Down to the physiological level, music takes hold of us. We might gravitate toward our favorite music for a variety of reasons. Think of your favorite song and some of its features that make you love it. Perhaps the lyrics speak to you in a profound way or remind you of a very happy memory. Maybe its rhythm and tone somehow lift your spirits without you even knowing how to explain that effect. My favorite song is Eric Clapton's "Tell Me that You Love Me" from his album *Backless*. When my wife and I were still dating, it played on the radio, and when I told her that it is my favorite, she replied, "This should be our song." Well, then I needed to marry her all the more out of fear of marring my favorite track. Joking aside, I appreciate the song and have a fond memory attached. Whatever reasons jump to your mind, undoubtedly the *melody* appeals to you. Clapton's guitar riff in "Tell Me that You Love Me" was the determinative factor in my initial affection for it. Importantly, melodies as melodies teach us something about our life with God as depicted in the creation account.

Unsurprisingly, melodies remind us of truths that the Genesis narrative has prompted us to consider concerning God himself. First, a properly melodic tune must have good *order*. Perhaps in a unique way when we use music to praise God, that worship reminds us of our point that God is the author of order. Second, a properly ordered melody needs to be *beautiful*. It must be pleasing. To meet both these requirements, a melody must have a satisfying resolution. Your favorite song would not be your favorite song if the primary measure's final note went up instead of down. Melodies must rightly resolve.

The same principle applies to our communion with God, so that the melody of our properly ordered life with the Lord requires the right resolution. We ought to be carried upon the right notes of reflecting the character of the God who made us to represent him, but the ultimate note of the harmony between the original and the image needs to resolve in the restful communion of worship. This chapter explores the main point that God consecrated his day of restful worship to show that his image bearers were made for everlasting communion with him.

THE SABBATH PRINCIPLE

You love *someone*—maybe a spouse, a child, a parent, a close friend. You have some special relationship that captures your affection and joy. When it comes to that person or those people, we have an intuitive sense that we do not need to find reasons to justify spending time with them. When I have told others that I am looking forward to a day of spending time with just my wife, no one has ever asked me why I am excited about that time together. It is obvious to everyone that I do not need any higher good than time with her since that time itself is often the goal of working toward a day off. If you go to one of your friends and propose getting together, but they respond "Why?" or "For what?" well, you know that there is a problem of some sort in that relationship. We intuitively know that time with those whom we most cherish needs no justification.

That simply spending time together with a loved one is a principle needing no defense shows how communion with others is itself inherently good. This good is not accidental because God created us for community, making being together itself a noble thing. In Genesis 2:18, God himself announced, "It is not good that the man should be alone." Notably, after God created man as male and female together, he declared that creation was "very good" (1:31). Now, several troubling cultural agendas as well as countless legitimately humorous jokes might prompt readers to focus on why it was not good for *man* to be alone, requiring the woman. But surely the emphasis is truly on how being *alone* was not good. In other words, God made humanity for community—made us for communion—entailing that fellowship is an end itself.

As our previous reflections upon the creation narrative have shown, Genesis 1 pushes us to recognize God's purposeful designs for creation. As the account develops, we see that day and night are meant to govern human patterns of work and rest, the land and sea form distinct habitats for land and sea creatures, and the sun and moon serve to mark the progression of time. The passage of time is not a superficial feature of the world. Just like the other features that God wove into creation, the means to track time serves a particular purpose.

The key importance of God appointing the means to monitor the progress of time relates to how God also purposed special time for our special purpose of communion with him. That purpose to track time's passing crucially mark creation's culmination in the Sabbath.

> Thus the heavens and the earth were finished, and all the host of them. And on the seventh day God finished his work that he had done, and he rested on the seventh day from all his work that he had done. So God blessed the seventh day and made it holy, because on it God rested from all his work that he had done in creation. (Genesis 2:1–3)

As the previous chapter considered, God created humanity with the purpose that we who are made in God's image would represent and reflect him within creation. Just like when you look in the mirror expecting to see the image look like you rather than a green elephant, so too God made humanity so that we refract his goodness within the world. Still, he never intended this reflection to occur in any sort of distant, detached sense but specifically within the context of our relationship of special communion with him. As it is not good that man should be alone, communion is built into our very nature.

We are, moreover, properly *and ultimately* ordered toward a specific communion, namely communion in restful worship with our God. The creation week progressed as God himself went through the specific pattern of working for the day and ceasing for the evening. This routine culminated at the end of the creation week as God consecrated a full day for the purpose of resting from his work. Now, God is impassible and does not genuinely tire from his acts within creation. His works within the world do not drain his energy since he is inexhaustible life itself. God did not even need to use time to conduct his creative work, being able to do all things at once by his sheer power if he had wanted. Because God is beyond getting tired, not needing to rest for the night to recover his strength, we know that his pattern of resting at the end of each creation day is also part of how Genesis addresses God's covenant people about our life with him.

God's practice of setting apart this day for rest sets a moral example for his people to imitate. He made humanity in his image to refract his goodness in creation not only through the things we do and the character we have but also by joining him in his rest. God's image bearers are not meant to be disconnected from the original but are meant to go forth as God's representatives into the world *and to* return for restful communion in worship. In other words, the image was made for the original and to be the recipient of everlasting blessed fellowship.

The Sabbath principle is that we were made for this communion in restful worship, building the Sabbath precept into creation. As the creation narrative progresses, revealing God's intentions for a properly ordered creation, God creates humanity with the purpose of representing him at the creaturely level within the world. This is one high point in the story as it shows God's intention for his character to be reflected within creation. Nonetheless, his full purposes culminate in consecrating the Sabbath as a time marked for restful communion in worship between God and his image bearers.

THE SABBATH PROBLEM

The progression of the creation narrative then emphasizes that Sabbath rest is *the* high point, the climax, of God's purposes in making the universe and making humanity. Now, Christians do not always think about the Sabbath in the same way, sometimes disagreeing about what it means. Without going into all those disagreements, which are far outside our purposes here, the main way that we are considering the Sabbath is a principled rhythm that God built into creation so that we would use one day of the week in a special way to commune with him in restful worship. Just as it was not good for man to be alone concerning all of life in general, it is not good for us to be alone for this special worship either, so Adam and Eve—as a model for us even today—participated in this restful worship as the corporate people of God.

Creation's Sabbath principle should capture more of our imagination than it often has. After all, our present focus is not on any sort of ceremonies or rituals that were introduced first under the Mosaic covenant. We are reflecting on the Genesis narrative to see how the principle of setting aside special time for communion with God and his people was woven into the fabric of creation. Many have rejected the notion of a creation Sabbath by raising "problems" about the complexity of relating God's consecration of the seventh day to the later command in the Ten Commandments delivered atop Mount Sinai and to a principled day of worship in general. This rejection, however, seems to focus too clinically on the early Genesis narrative, not giving due attention to how *Moses* authored this account for Israel's benefit as they reckoned with entering covenant life with God and not leaving room for the legitimate theological reflection that holy Scripture intends to prompt. From the contextual footing of an Israelite receiving the Ten Commandments announced from Sinai or later living under the Mosaic covenant, hearing this creation narrative about God's consecration of the seventh day would not trigger a list of intellectual complexities but signal how the moral law given to them, including the principle of a day for restful worship, was part of the true God's plan for his covenant creatures.

The true assertion of Scripture's objective meaning can be carried too far to squeeze out God's intent for Scripture to produce a subjective response. When we focus too surgically on lining up the continuity of Sabbath injunctions without recognizing the subjective force that the Genesis narrative should have for God's covenant people, we miss Scripture's principal exhortations. Moses's first readers would know that God commanded them to keep the Sabbath. When they heard the creation story, they would then recognize that God's reason for the Sabbath was not invented at Sinai but built into his purposes to have communion with us as his covenant creatures. The Genesis narrative as composed originally for God's people living the Mosaic covenant summoned Israel to participate in the creational gift of special time with God in worshipful rest. We hardly respond well to Scripture if we think that God no longer summons his covenant people to receive his gift of blessed time with him just because we no longer live under the specifically Mosaic form of keeping his moral law.

Regarding this simple idea that God was richly kind to us to grant us the gift of special time to commune with him in restful worship, we need to reflect more on this blessing of the Sabbath. As Hebrews 4:9 says, "there remains a Sabbath rest for the people of God," indicating how the Sabbath itself has abiding relevance for Christians. Many debates about whether Christians are obligated to keep the Sabbath miss the fundamental point that this day is given to us as a special gift from God. Too many evangelicals, as noted in our reflections upon what it means to bear God's image, focus on God's *commands* apart from *character* issues. For a good deal of Christians, the Sabbath relates to discovering the list of deeds to do or to avoid rather than to being a better bearer of God's image in a deeper sense.

Christians should not think about the Sabbath as a question of "What do I have to do?" We should not *reduce* our relationship with God to a list of dos and don'ts since godliness is a far more all-encompassing reality than the sum of our individual deeds. This reductionist way of thinking downgrades the Christian life from a full-orbed outlook about flourishing in pursuit of all that is good to simply rules about activities we should avoid. So, "Do I have to?" falls far short of the more ideal "What is good for me, and what orients me more fully toward communion with God?"

We know the reductionistic approach would fail in all our other relationships, marking it more plainly as wrongheaded regarding God. I cannot imagine how poorly it would go if I said to my wife, "Just let me know the list of what I have to do and what I cannot do to make you happy for our next date night." If I said that to her, it would write off the whole nature of that time as marked for communion and enjoyment of one another and reduce it to a non-relational checklist. If I said to my young son, "Give me a list of things I need to do to complete 'daddy time' so that I can move on to the other things I'd like to do," I'd be rightly criticized as an uninvested father. Why in the world would we ever try to think of the day that God set apart for us to commune with him along these lines?

The Sabbath principle promotes that God's design for us by nature is to have communion with him. If we want to appeal to creation for issues like biblical marriage, as we rightly should, we should accept the full scope of creation principles as God wired them into our nature. The argument that God made marriage between man and woman is one appropriate appeal to nature. The full moral law is also ever binding even upon those who are saved as the guide for our walk with God. Still, nature also declares that we were made for communion with God especially concerning one day in seven. The Sabbath principle is stamped onto God's creation purposes and even creation's culmination.

The Sabbath principle highlights how many Christians have probably come to think of weekly worship together with God's people too much as something of optional relevance. There is a modern tendency to think of worship as entailing specific types of personal experience, which eventually flattens our view of church into whatever fills our "spiritual batteries." This outlook makes coming to church with God's people optional because this sort of worship is really *for you*, namely, to refill those batteries. On these premises, if our batteries feel full, church seems optional, since its primary function is my recharging. Christians start to believe that they can dispose of involvement in church and attend gathered worship only when they feel the need for a spiritual pick-me-up.

Even more problematic, this same tendency to view church as optional comes with another potential danger to view gathered worship itself as only one option for refilling those spiritual batteries. The feeling that the spiritual batteries are full can entail that church is not needed that week. In like manner, church becomes completely optional if I feel like a walk in the forest fills my spiritual batteries better than gathered worship. Ironically, the things that tend to replace church for filling our batteries are usually our hobbies. We might think, "I just meet God more when I ride my horse or watch the football game or play my video games than at church." In this instance, we have mistaken things that we might like to do for things that provide spiritual nourishment. Hardly ever do these substitutes unsettle the soil that cradles the roots of our sin. They let us wallow in the swamps of our wickedness without being confronted with the reality of the living God. They are activities that coddle us in our enjoyable lives rather than a true encounter with the living God. We confuse the enjoyment of God-given good gifts with worship, so become guilty of violating the first commandment as well as the fourth.

We need to remember that God designed us with a purpose, properly ordered for communion with him. We have thought repeatedly about how our sin clips the wires of our heart from the way they should be ordered and reattaches them so that the electrical currents of our soul power wickedness rather than worship. When it comes to the principles that undergird the regular gathering of God's people to worship the Lord as an assembly, we again need to remember that when we begrudgingly drag ourselves to worship, we have forgotten our properly ordered purpose. The principle that God made the Sabbath for man, not man for the Sabbath, is certainly true but does not mean that he made it for us to use any way that sounds fun (Mark 2:23–28). The Sabbath was made for man so that we have the promised, guaranteed opportunity to commune with our God in the way that he intended for us from the beginning. Jesus certainly removed any burdens that Israel's ceremonial laws added but surely commends, as he supplies, the blessings for which the Sabbath was intended.[1]

In the modern world, this commitment to weekly worship according to God's pattern of worship is perhaps especially difficult concerning our kids. Parents sometimes complain that kids cannot pay attention throughout a long worship service. The default complaint from kids themselves, however, is often that church is boring or does not seem relevant. This is another version of the tendency to see church as having optional relevance. The preference for a few extra hours to play video games is certainly not because they are relevant to young people's lives in any meaningful sense. Video games and cartoons are not actually relevant but merely good at *distracting* us. We like to be distracted—to be pulled out of reality—but distractions are not really fulfilling. This is the same as our preference for junk food over steak. These things turn us into human marshmallows, adding no substance. We may be full but are not nourished.

The key to overturning this mindset, regardless of how old we might be, is to realize what worship truly is. I plead with Christian parents to think hard about this issue and not to indulge these complaints if your children make them. Rather, let us all remind ourselves that gathered worship coheres with creation's Sabbath principle that God has blessed a special time for extraordinary communion with his people. God's presence is not a boring or a trivial matter, so gathered worship is neither optional nor irrelevant if we understand that it is the time that God has appointed for us to encounter him in blessed fellowship. Far from distracting us from reality, worship engages us with the most meaningful activity we can have. We must all recover and reinforce the majesty of gathering to praise the true God since he has promised to meet his people.

There is a particular urgency in applying this appreciation to our children as we raise them in the faith. When I served as an assistant pastor in Northern Ireland and was heavily involved with ministering to the church's youth, my experience was that most of them could well digest a worship service, understanding and appreciating its flow from adoring God to confessing sin to knowing our pardon and hearing the gospel, and take away the substance of a full sermon ... *if that was expected of them.* If parents thought worship was boring, kids would too. If parents thought it was best to skip church for football, kids learned and preferred that practice pretty quickly as well. The parents' approach to worship and how much they followed up to ask their kids about what they digested from a worship service played the supreme role in how kids thought about church.

Furthermore, this urgency to raise children in the faith exhorts those who lead worship to remember that our task is not boring. Worship is not entertainment, so the task of leading it is certainly not built around amusing the congregation or even the children. Still, an encounter with the living God is an exciting event. Reverence, order, and decorum do not require stodginess, monotony, and lifelessness. For the sake of our children, and for ourselves, we who lead worship should convey how it is a privilege, a delight, and an anticipated blessing to gather in the Lord's presence.

Accordingly, for all our sakes, we should remind ourselves about how wonderful it is that God built the creation with a pinnacle point of time that God consecrated for restful worship to commune with his people. We especially push against the notion of letting our kids skip worship for other entertaining things—whether provided by the church itself or happening outside the church—hoping that later in life they will mystically learn to love gathered worship in the church. Even pragmatically, we do not take that approach with any other issue. No one thinks that if they do not make their kid eat vegetables rather than dessert for eighteen years, a switch flips when they go to university so that they love vegetables. I had to be taught to love vegetables. We need to train our kids to love what is good for them, which foremost includes worshipping God. Ask kids questions about worship. Engage them in conversation. If kids see you pay attention and care, they learn that.

As to worship's relevance, our primary purpose as God's image bearers is communion with our God, making the culminating point of our week in restful worship the most relevant activity we have since we were made for it. Too often, we look for worship to achieve *something else* besides communing we God. Maybe we expect church to equip us to transform the world or just to entertain us. Either way, communing with God becomes a tool instead of the goal. But time with him is the goal and must be the all-encompassing vision for our lives. As Westminster Shorter Catechism question 1 says, "Man's chief end is to glorify God, and to enjoy him forever."[2] The sum of our Sabbath problem is so often that we pretend that we were made for something other than this communion in restful worship in God's blessed presence.

THE SABBATH PROMISE

Despite obstacles that we may face concerning the Sabbath principle, including heart issues that may cause us to reckon with various issues of sanctification, the rich promise embedded in it is that God designed us and ordered us for communion with him. The heart issues may be daunting but are certainly not new, as we have always had difficulties in committing ourselves to our primary purpose of glorifying God. Even from the beginning, Adam himself preferred the devil's offer of forbidden fruit over everlasting blessed communion with God, leaving a terribly corrupting precedent wherein we prefer this world to that communion through participation in Sabbath worship.

Nonetheless, the Sabbath principle provides hope for Christians because it promises God's commitment to be joined with his people. The Sabbath always promised that joyous communion with God, continuing that promise even today, but now further promises the help to overcome those heart issues that make it hard for us to love worship in the first place. The point about God's ordinary means of grace again becomes pertinent because just as God consecrated one day of the week for communion with him, he has also consecrated the activities of worship to communicate blessings to us and even reshape our hearts so that we learn to prioritize communion with God again. In this respect, Westminster Shorter Catechism question 88 teaches, "The outward and ordinary means whereby Christ communicates to us the benefits of redemption are, his ordinances, especially the Word, sacraments, and prayer; all which are made effectual to the elect for salvation."[3] Although the Scripture being read and preached, the administration of baptism and the Lord's Supper, and praying are incredibly ordinary things, just like a day of the week is, God has promised to use these things as means for us to have blessed communion with him.

The creation Sabbath's promised rest is itself special and blessed. Did you notice in Genesis 2:1–3 that the seventh day does not end? The account of this day, unlike the other six, has no refrain of morning and evening. The reason for that omission is that God finished his work and so entered *unending* rest. God's entrance into that rest prepares that rest for us. If Adam had fulfilled the law, he would have joined God in that unending restful communion. Adam sinned, though, blocking our way to joining God in his perfect rest. We considered already how the creation principle means that the Sabbath is a precept for us, but we also need to see how it is still a promise for us, even in salvation. In the new covenant, we experience Christ's fulfillment of the Sabbath, not in some supposed nullification of the benefit of having one day in seven to commune with God in worship but by knowing that Christ has secured unending, eschatological rest for his people in the age to come.

The Bible provides a rationale to see the creation Sabbath as the source of this ongoing promise, even this side of the fall and especially as Christians looking forward to everlasting life. The fourth commandment provides some insight into this promise's abiding validity, especially as God revealed it to Israel twice. In Exodus 20:8–11, God stated the fourth commandment on the stone tablets as he made a covenant with Israel at Mount Sinai. In this case, he grounded the Sabbath precept in a specific way: "For in six days the Lord made heaven and earth, the sea, and all that is in them, and rested on the seventh day. Therefore the Lord blessed the Sabbath day and made it holy." This time, God appealed to his work of creation, specifically referring to the creation principle of worship as the Sabbath. As Israel prepared to enter the promised land, they considered the law again. In Deuteronomy 5:12–15, God again appealed to the creation principle to observe the Sabbath but further explained: "You shall remember that you were a slave in the land of Egypt, and the LORD your God brought you out from there with a mighty hand and an outstretched arm. Therefore the LORD your God commanded you to keep the Sabbath day." Far from being contradictory, competing, or contrasting points, the Bible shows that God orders humanity toward restful communion with him in worship by creation *and* redemption.[4] God created us for communion with him, and he has also redeemed us for communion with him.

For Christians, creation's unending Sabbath that offered the opportunity to join God in everlasting rest then remains an offer of hope for us. As Hebrews 4:9–10 explains, "So then, there remains a Sabbath rest for the people of God, for whoever has entered God's rest has also rested from his works as God did from his." Those who enter God's rest will cease from their work as he did, namely in permanent rest. The trouble for us is that although God finished his work and entered rest, sinners cannot even begin our work. We have spit in our Maker's face and thrown boulders in the pathway that he made for us to join him in everlasting communion. Sinners cannot enter our rest by our works.

Gladly, God has provided a way for us to join him in that promised rest by someone else's work. As Hebrews 4:14 says, "Since then we have a great high priest who has passed through the heavens, Jesus, the Son of God, let us hold fast our confession." Jesus has done the work required to obtain rest, and he has repaved the pathway that we destroyed. He has thrown open the doors to heaven if only we would walk through them by taking hold of the Savior by faith. If we cast ourselves upon him, his death pays for our sin and his resurrection is the pledge of our everlasting life. In his grace, God not only grants us access to restful communion with him as we gather on his day, but he also even uses that very communion toward which we were ordered to reorder us in our very hearts. By the Spirit's power through the ordinary means of grace, God rewires our poorly wired hearts so that we can once again cherish our time in God's presence rather than longing for the things of this world. Because of all that Christ has accomplished, the day of rest changed from the last day of the week to the first day of the week. Rather than working toward our rest with God, as it was for Adam, we work out of our rest with God, having already been fully received but now commissioned to serve him in gratitude.

One of the deacons at my church, Doug Vos, once helped me clarify a Sunday school lesson about the importance of Lord's Day worship. He said, "Worship is the closest that we get to heaven in this age." Doug was right. Although God is with us throughout our whole lives, Jesus promised to be specially present among his people where even just two or three gather in his name (Matthew 18:20). The church's precious blessing of Christ's presence in our gatherings just points forward to what life in the new creation will be like in every moment. In the age to come, we will know the direct presence of God in blessing in every moment of life in a way that we cannot even imagine in this era before the resurrection. The closest we can get to that new creation experience is in the gathering of God's people as the time that God has set apart to meet us.

When I lived in London, some streets were noticeably lined with embassies of other countries. The United States of America has embassies scattered all around the world. When the United States establishes an embassy, that plot of land becomes American soil. That section of earth is part of the United States even though it exists outside its natural borders. Christ's kingdom also has embassies spread across the earth: the church. To be sure, I do not mean the brick-and-mortar meeting houses that congregations own or rent, nor the plots of land on which those buildings reside. The embassy of the kingdom of heaven is Christ's people, gathered in his name for worship. When the call to worship goes forth, that assembly becomes heavenly soil. It becomes an outpost of the new creation, existing outside its natural borders that presently divide heaven and earth but nonetheless making the heavenly kingdom present on earth. Rather than a specific plot of land, God gives his people a time in which his kingdom protrudes into this age. His gives us the Sabbath, the day of rest, the space of moments in which we are caught up into his throne room as he inhabits our praises and communes with his people.

CONCLUSION

The Sabbath as the final note of the creation week makes the melody of God's purposes for us resolve. He ordered us to communion with him, and that communion finds its richest harmony in the ringing satisfaction of basking in God's presence on the day that he set apart to encounter him in restful worship. We live in a massively disordered world, dealing almost daily with a central crisis concerning identity. Every single message that our world throws at us screams for us to define ourselves by worldly standards, whether it be job, money, relationships, or the brands we use. In this light, the Sabbath as a time for communion with God is such a rich blessing as we *get to* set the world aside and *get to* abstain, yes, from pursuing our work since we cannot earn our Sabbath rest by them but also from all our commercial endeavors as a way to unload ourselves from the entirety of the worldly kingdom. After all, we cannot find identity in our purchases, politics, or even personalities but only in that God has called us into being as his image bearers who are made for communion with him. The promise of restful communion with God in worship, therefore, is the fitting final note of the human melody. The tune of our lives finally makes sense when viewed in light of the regular encounter that we have with our God on the day that he has appointed. The melody of human existence resolves as we find ourselves in the throne room of our God, welcomed because of Christ.

QUESTIONS FOR FURTHER REFLECTION

1. How does God's creation of Adam and then Eve show us that we were made to be in fellowship with God's people?

2. How does the Sabbath pattern seen in creation show us our highest goal is communion with God?

3. Why are we often tempted to view Sabbath worship as optional and confuse other activities as alternatives to meeting with God and his people?

4. Whether we have children or not, how can we encourage the covenant children in our congregations and teach and model for them the importance of regular worship?

5. How does our weekly Sabbath worship remind us of our promised eternal rest? For the believer living after the cross, what is the significance of our week beginning with our Sabbath rest?

6. Why and in what ways is it a complete confusion of categories and of where our highest blessing is to think it is alright to skip church for so-called "special occasions," such having NFL or NASCAR tickets?

7. How else do the ideas from this chapter help you determine what a good (and bad) use of the Lord's Day is?

8 A PLACE FOR COMMUNION

The Garden in Eden

You have to arrange several necessary things in order to make plans to be together with your friends and loved ones. First, getting together requires that you know *when* you will meet. If you do not know what time to get together, you are unlikely to cross paths. Although it can be difficult, we must *make time* in our schedules for *this time* together. Even if we put all that effort into managing our schedules, we might easily overlook something just as important as *when* to meet, namely, *where* to meet. If we do not set the location for getting together, we are just as unlikely to cross paths as if we never set a date. For fellowship together, we must remember that we need both *time* and *place*.

The point to see in Genesis' description of the garden of Eden is that the garden was God's first temple and Adam was the first priest. When he created us, God knew that his earthly creatures would live bound by the limitations of space and time, especially since he formed us to live in these ways. The creation account shows how God met that twofold need for us to have communion with him. We previously considered from Genesis 2:1–3 how God made us in his image to be properly ordered toward the *time* that we spend with him by consecrating the Sabbath as that special although regular occasion for restful worship in communion with him. Having established that *time* for us to commune with him, the creation account in Genesis 2:4–14 shows how God also built a *place* for us to commune with him. More specifically, the various aspects of this special place show that God intended it for *religious* fellowship between God and humanity, meaning that Adam's role in Eden facilitated our communion with the Lord as he tended the garden. This chapter explores this main point that God provides a place for his people to have communion with him.

THE PROVISION

The account in Genesis 2:4–14 records how God built the garden of Eden may seem like a report of a building site, focused on interests that may be fairly foreign to our own, but it plays a crucial role in sharpening the text's description of humanity's communion with God. In verses 4–9, the first section of this building site directs our attention to some significance concerning why God groomed this garden. Fundamentally, the construction and placement of the garden of Eden marks God's abundant provision in providing his people with a place for communion with him.

The narrative of Genesis 1–2 has progressively built as a continuous story so far but now pauses to reset the developing account. This new section begins:

> These are the generations
> of the heavens and the earth when they were created,
> in the day that the Lord God made the earth
> and the heavens. (Genesis 2:4)

The significance of this part of the narrative lies in Genesis' repeated use of the phrase "these are the generations of" as a structural device showing the story's major divisions concerning the generations of various figures within the history, for example, "This is the book *of the generations of* Adam" (5:1) or "These are the generations of Noah" (6:9). This structural device appears ten times throughout the book (2:4; 5:1; 6:9; 10:1; 11:10, 27; 25:12, 19; 36:1, 9; 37:2).[1] Genesis 2:4 then signals that creation's prologue has ended, and chapter one is beginning. Whereas the prologue focused on creation's universal scope, this section attends more closely to the first events of human history, rewinding slightly to give more detail about what happened on the sixth day.[2]

Despite the structural cue, signaling a new section with a closer focus on events already mentioned, the story develops further in thematic continuity. Primarily, the whole narrative of Genesis 1–2 focuses on humanity's communion with God, this new section providing greater detail about the nature of that communion, first highlighting the place God provided to meet with his people, directly after the account of the time he consecrated to meet us. More specific to the literary development, the prologue set the stage by providing knowledge of God's universal work of creation, informing us that he was the Maker of everything that exists, even as this new section zooms in to consider a particular location on earth.

In that respect, our attention narrows from the whole universe to a particular land where plants are about to grow. The context is set in verse 5: "When no bush of the field was yet *in the land* and no small plant of the field had yet sprung up—for the Lord God had not caused it to rain on the land, and there was no man to work the ground." Note that this is establishing a time frame for *when* God would build the garden. Specifically, although God had already *made* the plants (1:11–13), they had not yet sprouted in *this land*. So, although existing, they had not yet grown *here*, explaining why Genesis 1 and 2 do not contradict each other regarding the order in which God created plants and humans.[3] Two reasons then ground why plants were not yet in this land.

First, God had not yet caused it to rain *on this land*. We saw in Genesis 1:6–8 how God created the clouds as the upper waters, entailing creation's two normal features that rain is a constant natural resource and plants need rain.[4] That it had not rained *in this land* also indicates the time of year these events occurred. In the ancient Near East, summer was the dry season and winter was the wet season. Although Genesis has clearly depicted God as establishing the normal patterns of weather, biblical authors like Moses recognized that God is ultimately sovereign over the seasons and rainfall.[5] Even while affirming the normal seasonal patterns, we still believe that God is the one who brings rain in wet seasons.[6] The plants had not yet grown in this land where God would build the garden because rain had not yet fallen.

Second, the other reason that plants had not yet grown *in this land* was that people had not irrigated it. The reason why people were not there to work the ground is obvious at this juncture in the narrative: God had not created them yet.[7] This portion of the story has rewound to provide greater insight into the events of the sixth day, so we are reading about the situation before God formed humanity.

The story progresses as the twofold problem of no rain and no farmer receives a twofold solution.[8] The first confirms that these events took place near the wet season because "a mist was going up from the land and was watering the whole face of the ground" (2:6). This Hebrew word translated "mist" occurs in only one other place, shedding light on its meaning. Job 36:27–28 reads,

> For he draws up the drops of water;
> they distill his mist in rain,
> which the skies pour down
> and drop on mankind abundantly.

This "mist" is then simply a raincloud that God made rise to water the ground, not some mysterious weather phenomenon lingering from the earth's previous oversaturation with water.[9] This raincloud is not surprising, given that God installed this natural function into nature on the second day. After all, the problem was not lack of general water but lack specifically of *rain*.[10]

The narrative focuses precisely on this particular timeframe, featuring that twofold problem to signal that something is about to happen. The approaching wet season, entailing the expectation of growth and new life, not only addresses the first problem of a lack of rain but also builds anticipation. The story satisfies our anticipation by revealing that the expected new life is actually human life as God creates the first man, Adam: "then the LORD God formed the man of dust from the ground and breathed into his nostrils the breath of life, and the man became a living creature" (2:7). After creating Adam, God planted a garden in Eden and put Adam there:

> And the LORD God planted a garden in Eden, in the east, and there he put the man whom he had formed. And out of the ground the LORD God made to spring up every tree that is pleasant to the sight and good for food. The tree of life was in the midst of the garden, and the tree of the knowledge of good and evil. (2:8–9)

Interestingly, God made Adam somewhere *else* other than Eden. Even then, Eden is a larger place inside which God planted the garden, then took Adam from that other place to put him in paradise.

These particular details of the story significantly underline God's special provision for Adam as his special creature. Adam's creation outside Eden is not incidental nor accidental to the story or its significance. This passage emphasizes that regardless of where on earth God first made Adam, he carefully selected and prepared a special place for Adam to live. He did not just build the garden around Adam but chose the best place to provide a home for his image bearer. Further and more importantly, God did not leave Adam to make his own dwelling but built one for him, made it abundant for food and provision, and guided him to it. After all, Adam was a real person and so would need a real place to dwell. God was good in making that place for him, showing that God's gift was the provision of a wonderful home for his people to dwell.

Already the story of God making the garden for Adam teaches us something of our need to trust God's providence. We often get very ingrained and settled where we are. We typically do not like change. God, however, knows best where we will thrive, know his presence most closely, and be most useful. We are never in a particular place in life by accident. After all, God made Adam in one spot, knowing full well that he would build Eden and relocate Adam there. Sometimes, God needs to move us from where he once placed us to put us where we most belong in his purposes now. Israel would not have missed that point as they read Genesis 1–2, knowing that God once placed them in Egypt to help them thrive under Joseph's reign (Genesis 46:1–47:12) but now, as he inspired Moses to write Genesis, had freed them from Egyptian slavery. God was behind both relocations for his people's good. As we recognize God's patterns with Adam and Israel, we learn to trust that as God opens doors—sometimes having to shove us through them—he is working for our good and his glory as he moves us from one place, phase, or position in life to another.

THE PRIEST

The Genesis story shows that God gave Adam a home but also that this home had a special purpose. This garden of Eden was to be the place devoted to worshipful communion with God.[11] For this reason, rather than providing archeologists with a mystical treasure map, the description of Eden is intricately detailed:

> A river flowed out of Eden to water the garden, and there it divided and became four rivers. The name of the first is the Pishon. It is the one that flowed around the whole land of Havilah, where there is gold. And the gold of that land is good; bdellium and onyx stone are there. The name of the second river is the Gihon. It is the one that flowed around the whole land of Cush. And the name of the third river is the Tigris, which flows east of Assyria. And the fourth river is the Euphrates. (Genesis 2:10–14)

Christians know that God is present everywhere but also that God makes himself specially present in blessing in certain places and times, as in Eden.

The description of Eden's location provides the evidence that the garden was a place of special communion with God. First, Scripture regularly features God using mountains for major covenantal events, such as covenanting with Israel atop Mount Sinai or securing the new covenant in Christ's death atop Mount Calvary.

Scripture also presents Eden as a mountain. The prophet Ezekiel explicitly confirms Eden's mountainous location:

> *You were in Eden, the garden of God;*
> every precious stone was your covering,
> sardius, topaz, and diamond,
> beryl, onyx, and jasper,
> sapphire, emerald, and carbuncle;
> and crafted in gold were your settings
> and your engravings.
> On the day that you were created
> they were prepared.
>
> You were an anointed guardian cherub.
> I placed you; you were on the holy mountain of God;
> in the midst of the stones of fire you walked.
> (Ezekiel 28:13–14)

Within the stated context of "Eden, the garden of God," the creation of man explicitly mentions how God put him on a mountain. The details of the Genesis narrative confirm the point. The direction of the rivers all flowing out of Eden suggests that they flowed downhill, placing the location atop a mountain. Further, the new Jerusalem, so clearly reflecting Eden's paradise, has a river flowing from it, being connected to a high mountain (Revelation 21:10–11; 22:1).[12] As God regularly made covenants with his people atop mountains, Eden was another mountain where God provided his presence in special blessing.

The description of Eden's location certainly marks it as a real place somewhere but more importantly indicates Eden's *function*. As Scripture associates abundant water with God's temple, the temple being the place of God's special presence with his people, the multiple rivers around Eden mark a place with abundant flowing water (Ezekiel 43:2; 47:1–12).[13] Moses mentioned these four rivers certainly because they were real, even if we no longer know where the Pishon and Gihon were, but moreover to tie Eden to temple imagery. This imagery intensifies when we notice that Israel had a *seven-day* process for dedicating the temple, linking this section and its description of the place of our communion with God more deeply into the overall creation narrative (1 Kings 8:65; 2 Chronicles 7:9).[14] More than any scientific theory, especially later Israelites would have immediately connected Moses's creation account with *worship*, associating the seven days leading up to the consecration of his cosmic Sabbath to the seven days leading up to the consecration of their temple.

The stones listed in Eden—gold, bdellium, and onyx—also draw connections to the garden as a place of worship.[15] In Exodus 28:6–10, God instructed Israel concerning how to make the priestly garments:

> And they shall make the ephod of gold, of blue and purple and scarlet yarns, and of fine twined linen, skillfully worked. It shall have two shoulder pieces attached to its two edges, so that it may be joined together. And the skillfully woven band on it shall be made like it and be of one piece with it, of gold, blue and purple and scarlet yarns, and fine twined linen. You shall take two onyx stones, and engrave on them the names of the sons of Israel, six of their names on the one stone, and the names of the remaining six on the other stone, in the order of their birth.

Crucially, gold and onyx, notably present in Eden, were necessary fixtures of the priestly garment. Indeed, even Ezekiel mentions gold and onyx in his description of God's mountaintop garden. Further, apart from Genesis 2:12, Scripture mentions bdellium only as a description of the manna that God provided as food for the Israelites as he traversed the wilderness with them. Some of this manna was then kept in the ark of the covenant in the Holy of Holies in the temple's innermost part.[16] Although Moses could have written about any number of natural resources near Eden, he drew attention to those that forged a link between Eden and the priestly role and the temple.

Even God's care for the garden surrounding Adam's work in and exile from it marks it with more temple imagery. In Genesis 2:15, "The Lord God took the man and put him in the garden of Eden to work it and keep it." The Hebrew words translated "work" and "keep" appear elsewhere together concerning the priestly task to "to serve and to guard" the temple (e.g., Exodus 36:8; Numbers 3:6–8; 18:5–6; Ezekiel 44:14), marking Adam's role as a priest in the garden.[17] Priests, however, were those who could enter directly into God's presence and commune with the Lord during their service in the temple. In Genesis 3:24, God appointed cherubim to guard Eden after Adam's fall. Throughout Scripture, cherubim function to guard God's presence in the tabernacle (Exodus 26:1; 36:35), in the Solomonic temple (1 Kings 6:22–24), and even atop the ark of the covenant itself (Exodus 25:17–22;; 37:7–9).[18] Thus, the garden in Eden was God's first temple and Adam his first priest. In other words, the description of Eden's location consistently marked the garden as a place of worship, a place where God met his people, spoke directly with them, and walked with them in unbroken and perfect fellowship. God built the garden specifically in Eden not only so that Adam would have a home, since that could have been anywhere, but to mark it with his special presence, putting Adam there to be the priest who had communion with him in the holy of holies.

THE PRESENCE

Adam's priestly role to tend God's first temple, marked with the Lord's special presence, does not indicate that the garden's specific location was meant to be a permanent limitation. Rather, Adam had an opportunity concerning the garden and God's presence, which continues to offer good news and promises to us today. Remember that one task that God gave to Adam as the priest who worked and kept the garden temple was from Genesis 1:28: "Be fruitful and multiply and fill the earth and subdue it." The priestly task to work and keep the garden also meant to expand the garden so that it covered the earth. In other words, the place of God's special presence was meant to fill the world. It was an opportunity for Adam's ministry in multiplying God's image with Eve and turning the whole world into a sacred space for God's image bearers to commune with their Lord.

The problem is that Adam made the world into a *sinful* rather than a *sacred* space. In this respect, God, who is infinitely holy, cannot justly stand to allow those who are wicked into his blessed presence. Just like Adam should have killed and cast out the serpent who wickedly invaded the sacred space, so too God owes death and ejection to everyone who violates the terms of his covenant with his image bearers.[19] Because God is inherently good, his righteousness demands that he end the presence of any wickedness before him, leaving everyone under God's impending curse. Everyone who has sinned, has broken God's law, has fallen short of righteousness at all, has failed to reflect God's image perfectly teeters under a death sentence for this life and the next.

In his mercy, however, God has given a stay of execution. Instead of killing Adam and throwing his corpse out of Eden, he exiled him back into the world outside the sacred space made for communion with God. We too still wander this land outside that blessed garden as exiles and pilgrims who were made for more but linger in lostness. Most pointedly, death amounts to exile from God's blessed presence.[20]

God's mercy extends all the more in offering a promise of restoration. Even in Israel, God renewed the promise of a *place* for communion with him. In a provisional way, God gave Jerusalem to them, describing it in Edenic terms: "There is a *river* whose streams make glad the city of God, the *holy habitation* of the Most High. *God is in the midst of her*" (Psalm 46:4–5). In the fullness of time, though, God sent forth his Son to bear the curse of the law and redeem us who were under that curse (Galatians 4:4–7). In Christ, God has made communion with him globally accessible.

As God then reopens the door to having a place to commune with him, the tension is that Christ's kingdom is not yet physically present on earth. In this sense, his kingdom remains not of this world (John 18:36). Still, Christ promises that the place where he will now be truly although spiritually present with us is in the church: "Where two or three are gathered in my name, there am I among them" (Matthew 18:20). As the church gathers, he is among us, confirming that even the smallest church is genuinely in communion with God, the emphasis being that *wherever* the church gathers, Christ is present to commune with us.

God provides a place for us to commune with him in the church, but his presence is not tied to one city, one temple, one building, or one garden. The church is the place for communion with God not as walls or a steeple but as the formal gathering of God's people in worship. God consecrated the time of the Sabbath to promise his communion but has also promised us a place to meet him among his people, as we meet in Christ's name under the preached Word.

Christian, God has always built a home for his people, and God still builds a home for his people. No matter where you are from or what your biological family is like, God builds the church so that you would be among your everlasting family. God has made a place for communion with you by meeting you personally in the church, but that place is among other believers. God shows you that he is with you by placing other Christians with you.[21] In this place for communion in the church, together as God's new creation *garden*, we may be individual trees, but like in any garden, we are meant to grow *together*, feeding off the same nutrients provided by the same gardener and lending a hand to one another as we grow in the same place. So the place for communion now is, very literally, a community.

We might also pause to note how in the creation context, God built a sacred space for his people where he *fed* them. The location of his concentrated presence in blessing was a garden where he gave Adam and Eve food to eat, save one tree. In other words, from the outset, God's sacred places were meant for eating. Even after the fall, God continues to provide food as a special blessing for his people. One of David's praises for God as his Shepherd is "You prepare a table before me in the presence of my enemies" (Psalm 23:5), highlighting that God's care for his servants still involves feeding them, even as we live in the fallen world.

In the new covenant, God forges his covenant community and sets a table for them as the hostile world swirls around us in the Lord's Supper. As in the garden of Eden, the church is God's covenantal sacred space where he feeds us. Jesus doubly commissioned Peter, representing the apostles as the foundation of the church (Ephesians 2:20), to "Feed my lambs" and "Feed my sheep" (John 21:15, 17). This commission certainly encompasses the whole pastoral task of caring for God's people, including preaching, prayer, and shepherding. Nonetheless, the encapsulating metaphor for all pastoral care focuses on food, pointing to the Lord's Supper as the fitting snapshot of all God's provision for his people in the new covenant. Paul rebuked the Corinthian church because "When you come together, it is not the Lord's supper that you eat" (1 Corinthians 11:20). Their coming together was the church's regular gathering on the Lord's Day, which was accompanied each week by the Lord's Supper.[22] Paul's criticism nearly entails that the problem with their worship was that their weekly gathering lacked the Lord's Supper, even though in their case they were trying but failing because of their inappropriate conduct at the meal. Biblically, the Lord's Supper was central to the church's life as God's covenant community (Acts 2:42).

In these days in which we wait between Christ's first and second comings, God still stages his sacred space as a place for eating. At creation, he planted a garden to meet Adam in special blessing and to feed him. In the church, he sets a table to mark his people out from the world as we proclaim Christ's death until he comes *by our eating* (1 Corinthians 11:26). God feeds us bread and wine, signifying and sealing how he feeds Christ himself to us as we receive him by faith (John 6:52–59). Our regular gathering around God's feast highlights how his presence with his people has always been marked by sacred eating. As he fed his community in Eden and feeds his people in the church, he promises still to set a feast for his people to feed us fully when Christ returns and we celebrate the wedding supper of the Lamb (Revelation 19:6–9).

Our present blessing pointing to that future feast sets forth a promise for a true place for communion that remains still ahead of us. One day, God's people will again have a spiritual and a physical place for communion that will also be universal. When Jesus returns, the new creation will envelop the globe with God's special presence for his people to commune with him.

The same themes that mark Eden as a sacred space develop across Scripture to indicate the expansion of the place of God's presence. In Revelation 21–22, the apostle John applies many of Eden's features in expanded form to the new Jerusalem as it descends from heaven to be the new home for God's people. As Eden was linked to God's mountain, the angel took John "to a great, high mountain" to see the new creation come down to earth (21:10). Like Eden had the rivers flowing from it, the new Jerusalem has "the river of the water of life, bright as crystal, flowing from the throne of God and of the Lamb through the middle of the street of the city" (22:1–2). Eden had an abundance of gold, and John sees how in the new Jerusalem "the city was pure gold ... and the street of the city was pure gold" (21:18, 21). Concerning the other stones near Eden, when Israel made the priestly garments, they included other stones in addition to gold and onyx, namely sardius, topaz, carbuncle, emerald, sapphire, diamond, jacinth, agate, amethyst, beryl, and jasper (Exodus 39:8–14). John records how these appeared as the materials of the new creation:

> The wall was built of jasper, while the city was pure gold, like clear glass. The foundations of the wall of the city were adorned with every kind of jewel. The first was jasper, the second sapphire, the third agate, the fourth emerald, the fifth onyx, the sixth carnelian, the seventh chrysolite, the eighth beryl, the ninth topaz, the tenth chrysoprase, the eleventh jacinth, the twelfth amethyst. And the twelve gates were twelve pearls, each of the gates made of a single pearl, and the street of the city was pure gold, like transparent glass. (Revelation 21:18–21)

The new Jerusalem is clearly depicted as the new Eden that expands to cover the earth. The presence of God becomes universal so that all people everywhere who trusted in Christ will have a true place to commune directly with God. God's dwelling place will be with his people, but his people will inherit the earth (Revelation 21:3).

CONCLUSION

Adam was supposed to fill and subdue the earth, thereby extending Eden's garden as the place of God's special presence across the world. God's presence, initially limited to Eden, would fill the globe. Where Adam failed, Christ succeeds. When Adam should have killed the serpent, Christ will kill the dragon (Revelation 20:4–10; 2 Thessalonians 2:8).[23] Those who remain in their sin will be thrown into the lake of fire with the devil and his angels, but for those with faith in Christ, those who have run to the Savior for the forgiveness of sin and reconciliation with God, the world will be God's temple. The whole earth will become the sacred space where God dwells with his people, the place for communion, so that everywhere we will bask in the full splendor of our God's loving presence.[24]

QUESTIONS FOR FURTHER REFLECTION

1. In our relationship with God, who initiates communion? Give specific examples of how this is demonstrated in God's relationship with Adam.
2. What biblical evidence supports the idea of the garden in Eden being a temple?
3. How did God create the garden to be both *functional* and *beautiful*?
4. As a priest, how was Adam to expand and fill the temple? How did sin corrupt this mandate and break communion with God?
5. How does the New Jerusalem correlate to and fulfill Eden?

COMMUNION BY COVENANT

A Trial by Trees

School takes up a lot of years in our lives. For most of us, we spend some twelve years, Monday to Friday from 8:00 a.m. to 3:15 p.m., pushing through classes as well as homework. The fine point on it all is that we end up taking a lot of exams over the course of our lives. Even after passing exams concerning the general studies everyone undertakes in those early years of school, we proceed to take more exams for whatever vocation God has given us. Whether we work in trades, ivory towers, or somewhere in between, we all go through the ordeal of passing some sort of exam to obtain qualifications for our work.

Now, exams provide genuine joy to only very few people, but they do exist for a reason. *Good* teachers examine their students not because they assume students are ignorant or will fail but because they want to give students the opportunity to demonstrate their ability. Good teachers examine students on the assumption that they can do it and should have the opportunity to showcase their performance. These opportunities allow students to confirm what they are able to do.

As God more pointedly defined Adam's priestly role in the garden, we see that same principle as God cements the structure of his relationship with humanity. Every analogy breaks down at some point, so we must not take the illustration of teachers examining their students to apply here as if God was confirming knowledge that Adam had learned. Rather, he was giving Adam the opportunity to demonstrate the ability *for righteousness* with which God equipped him as the divine image bearer. In Genesis 2:15–17, God instructed Adam about the content of his test of righteousness:

> The LORD God took the man and put him in the garden of Eden to work it and keep it. And the LORD God commanded the man, saying, "You may surely eat of every tree of the garden, but of the tree of the knowledge of good and evil you shall not eat, for in the day that you eat of it you shall surely die.

Our reflections on Genesis 1–2 have led us through God's work of properly ordering the universe, including forming us in his image to reflect him and meet him in the communion of worshipful rest. As God completed his work, he entered his never-ending Sabbath, implicitly offering us the opportunity to join him in it (Genesis 2:1–3). The question then becomes how we can join God in that unending rest.

By adding his command concerning the Tree of Knowledge of Good and Evil, this prohibition against one tree, God provided the means by which we could join him in that everlasting communion. God did not issue his prohibition against that tree, however, as if he assumed that his students—better, his covenant servants—were ignorant, needing to be found out. Instead, God built humanity with the inborn ability to reflect his goodness as those who are made in his image and so have everything that they would need to keep this command, had they chosen to do so.

This relationship wherein God offered Adam higher and everlasting blessings in connection with his obedience, specifically concerning the Tree of Knowledge of Good and Evil, returns our reflections to the idea of covenant. Namely, this test of Adam's obedience was part of God's covenant with him. Still, that God made Adam hardwired with original righteousness shows how the covenant he made with Adam was by no means an afterthought to his relationship with humanity. Although the Tree of Knowledge of Good and Evil was a special command, its role was to test Adam's natural abilities in righteousness. The covenant then centered on testing Adam's natural constitution and intensifying the experience of communion with God that humanity had by nature. The added command about the tree facilitated but did not create the covenant between God and Adam. This chapter reflects upon the main point that God has always offered the reward of incorruptible life and everlasting communion with him by way of covenant.

THE TREES

The creation narrative's earlier emphasis on vegetation has charged this account with some expectation concerning the role plants will play within the unfolding drama of our original communion with God. In Genesis 1, the usual pattern of God's creative work was to perform one major act for each day. God created light on day one, the expanse of the sky on day two, the lights to rule the sky on day four, and the sea and sky creatures on day five. The exceptions to this pattern, however, are days three and six, wherein God performed the one expected creative act but also supplemented it with another.

The breach of this pattern intentionally highlights that second act as critically important. For the second half of the week, focused on filling the earth, on day six, God created the animals but also formed man from the dust of the earth, installing him in creation as the divine image bearer. This supplemental creative act on day six, namely making humanity, was clearly a high point in the text but was noted as such not only by the content about the creatures made in God's likeness but also by the break with God's usual pattern of performing one creative act before ceasing work for the evening. The emphasis that God's break of pattern on day six places on humanity's creation suggests that his break from the pattern on day three also emphasizes his supplemental creative act. On day three, he first distinguished land and sea, then commanded the earth to sprout vegetation, each type yielding seed to reproduce according to its kind (Genesis 1:11–13). The first half of the creation week, which focused on forming the earth, culminated with an emphasis on the plants and how they reproduce normally.

God himself connected this supplemental act of making the vegetation on day three to the obviously emphatic work of creating humanity in his first address to his image bearers. As he explained to his newly created image bearers what it means for them to live according to his likeness, he brought attention to the plants: "Behold, I have given you every plant yielding seed that is on the face of all the earth, and every tree with seed in its fruit. You shall have them for food" (Genesis 1:29). The narrative introduces the gift of plants for food here to emphasize the role that plants play in the whole creation drama. This emphasis on plants' role foreshadows the key function of the Tree of Life and the Tree of Knowledge of Good and Evil within the covenant that God made with Adam.[1]

A covenant is simply a formal relationship. We make different sorts of covenants when we sign an agreement to buy a house, when we take a job and agree on our obligations and our rewards, and when we get married by legally promising that we will always love one another. These different relationships are all unquestionably binding. The diversity of these formal relationships is certainly important. A property contract is in essence a flat transaction with very little room in the agreement itself for any personal dynamics. On the other hand, a marriage's legal aspect functionally binds a man and woman to the personal dynamics of their relationship. It is inherently an intimate relationship, while also a formal and binding one. For a host of reasons, marriage is probably the closest example to illustrate how we should think about the covenants that God makes with his people. So, "covenant" may sound like a big theological word but simply indicates a relationship that is official and binding.

The creation narrative, especially in Genesis 2, presents God's relationship with Adam as a covenant relationship. One indication of this covenant between God and Adam is the particular uses of God's name within the creation account. Throughout Genesis 1:1–2:3, the Creator is called simply "God" or "Elohim," which is the general way to refer to God. Then, in Genesis 2:4, God is called "the LORD God" or "Yahweh Elohim." "Yahweh" is God's personal name (Exodus 3:14) or, better, the name by which his covenant people know him (Exodus 6:4–6). So, Yahweh as God's covenant name shows that this account is about God in covenant—an official relationship—with his people.[2]

Another indication is Adam's role as the priest in the garden-temple, which the previous chapter discussed at length. Considering the priesthood throughout Scripture, priests were always tied to covenants. This connection is most obvious under the Mosaic covenant as the Levitical priests served the Jerusalem temple inherently linked to the covenant order that God forged with Israel at Mount Sinai. Closer to us, Jesus is our high priest as the guarantor of the new covenant. The relationship of priests and covenants is partly spelled out as the letter to the Hebrews explains the transition from the Mosaic priesthood to Christ's. Drawing on God's declaration in Psalm 110:4 that appointed Christ as a priest forever, Hebrews says:

> This makes Jesus the guarantor of a better covenant. The former priests were many in number, because they were prevented by death from continuing in office, but he holds his priesthood permanently, because he continues forever. (Hebrews 7:22–24)

Jesus's position as the *covenant* guarantor is plainly joined to his permanent *priesthood*. Given the consistent connection between the priestly role and the covenant, Adam's role as a priest in the garden marks that he was the priest in a covenant with God.

Adam's covenantal relationship with God then raises the question concerning what this covenant was like. What was its content and the nature of the relationship forged in this covenant? We already reflected on some basic features of humanity's covenant relationship with God. First, we are made in his image, entailing our ethical obligation to show his goodness by acting in accord with his character. Second, God made us for everlasting communion with him. God consecrated the Sabbath to mark the time for communion with him, then built the garden in Eden as the place for communion with him. These two aspects of ethical obligation and special communion with God characterize the basic features of God's covenantal relationship with Adam. These features are the basic obligations and blessings of our covenant relationship with God.

In the creation account, the two special trees highlight and help explain those covenant obligations and blessings. In this covenant, God offered to reward Adam with even greater blessings than he possessed by creation but required Adam to render both general and focused obedience as the condition to obtain that reward. The Tree of Life indicates the offer of those greater blessings, but the Tree of Knowledge indicates the condition of focused obedience.

Although the next section focuses on the Tree of Knowledge of Good and Evil, we need to reflect first on the Tree of Life's significance in God's covenant with Adam. This tree spotlights God's generosity in that although Adam already had amazing blessings of a home in paradise and the enjoyment of blessed communion with the Lord in this first covenant, God in rich kindness offered to give even greater blessings to him. As God took Adam from wherever he had created him to place him in his new paradisiacal home, the story focuses on the trees' place in the garden: "The tree of life was in the midst of the garden, and the tree of the knowledge of good and evil" (Genesis 2:9). Both trees focus on some aspect of God's covenant with Adam, but the Tree of Life teaches about the reward that God offered to Adam in this covenant.[3]

The reward signified in the Tree of Life was heightened, deeper, incorruptible, everlasting communion with God. Now, clearly Adam's life was amazing and had none of the deficiencies that we experience because of our sin. This reward, far from diminishing what Adam had, simply indicates how God is so generous that he can always outgive himself, even in his most impressive gifts. To deepen the communion that Adam had with him in no way suggests that the first relationship wanted for anything but only indicates how God set out to be increasingly good to his servants as they fulfilled the tasks appointed for them.

To illustrate this idea, think about a family movie night. In this case, Dad instructs his son to clean his room before watching TV with the rest of the family. Additionally, he offers to give his son ice cream to eat during the movie if he cleans his room quickly. As part of the general contours of family communion, the son already had to fulfill the obligation of cleaning his room. Still, the father generously offers to sweeten that communion, as wonderful as it already was, if his son completes his obligation in a specific way. The special trees in the garden of Eden show that although God granted us communion with himself by making us in his image, he created us with the covenantal prospect of enjoying even higher blessings through the Tree of Life at the end of our work.

The Tree of Life pointed to the possibility for Adam to be confirmed in everlasting righteousness, guaranteeing him an incorruptible, glorified body. As we all should know, Adam would face the serpent's temptation to sin against God (Genesis 3:1–7). On the other side of that temptation, if Adam had been successful, he never would have faced temptation again. His situation would have been improved as God confirmed him in everlasting life. Adam had a wonderful life in Eden with all that he could want. Yet Adam had the possibility to disobey, fall into sin, and lose God's favor. The Tree of Life pointed to the life Adam could have had on the other side of that temptation if he had remained faithful to God.

The Tree of Life was then a sacramental sign of the covenant, symbolizing God's offer to Adam of greater blessings. A sacrament is just a feature of creaturely life that God specially uses to convey spiritual blessings to his people. In the new covenant, God has appointed water, a normal feature of creaturely life, for use in baptism to signify the cleansing and new life that we receive from Christ. Likewise, God has appointed bread and wine, ordinary elements of human meals, for use in a sacred meal in the church in which God's people commune together in worship to encounter our Lord. In his covenant with Adam, God appointed this Tree of Life to signify Adam's potential reward. For all we know, it had been a normal tree as one among the many but was now identified as special only by God's command. When God cast Adam and Eve out of the garden after they sinned, he explained his reason for exiling them: "lest he reach out his hand and take also of the tree of life and eat, and live forever" (Genesis 3:22). If Adam had eaten from this tree, he would have lived forever. The tree had no magical powers, but God had appointed it to signify Adam's everlasting life on the other side of his temptation. The tree sacramentally sealed God's offer of incorruptible, glorified, everlasting life in indestructible communion with God.

Amazingly, in contrast to how Adam needed to obtain the right to eat his sacramental meal at the consummation, God grants us the right to his table here and now this side of Christ's return. Those who eat in a worthy manner, namely with true faith, receive bread and wine as a pledge for their seat at the Lamb's wedding supper at the last day. Rather than working toward our sacred meal with the Lord, God uses our sacred meal to nourish us in grace and empower us for the Christian life.

THE TRIAL

God's command to Adam concerning the Tree of Knowledge of Good and Evil sharpens our understanding of its function as part of this first covenant.

> The LORD God took the man and put him in the garden of Eden to work it and keep it. And the LORD God commanded the man, saying, "You may surely eat of every tree of the garden, but of the tree of the knowledge of good and evil you shall not eat,

> for in the day that you eat of it you shall surely die." (Genesis 2:15–17)

Although Adam was naturally responsible to reflect God's image and to spread the garden kingdom across the earth, God assigned this extra command to focus the covenant directly upon Adam's obedience. The Tree of Knowledge was then the critical aspect of Adam's trial of obedience by which he could obtain unbreakable communion with him.

Perhaps you think that it seems odd that God would make a tree the test of Adam's obedience. One tree seems so insignificant when Adam could eat from them all (Genesis1:29). God's purpose in appointing this tree as Adam's trial of obedience was precisely because it was essentially an easy task, especially given Adam's natural righteousness (Ephesians 4:24; Colossians 3:10), that displayed very clearly whether Adam would decide to listen to God or disobey him. God assigned a simple tree as Adam's covenant test, to expose sin entirely for what it is: wicked rebellion against God. Geerhardus Vos took up this same issue, writing:

> What is the rationale for the probation command?
>
> That God made a morally neutral thing the point of decision appears, as was just noted, to have had the purpose of ridding sin of all incidental features and to lay it bare at its core. If man sinned against this command, then it could be for no other reason than that he choose evil and rejected good as good.[4]

Adam had nothing to gain but everything to lose by eating this one tree, since the tree itself was nothing more than the test of his commitment to God.

Adam's decision then related entirely to whether he would obey God or love evil. John Calvin explains:

> Moses now teaches that man was the governor of the world, with this exception, that nevertheless he should be subject to God. This law is assigned to him as a sign of his subjection since it would matter nothing to God if he had eaten whatever fruit he pleased. Therefore, the prohibition of the one tree was an examination of obedience ... Therefore, abstaining from the one tree's fruit was a certain kind of first lesson in obedience so that man might know he had a ruler of his life and Lord upon whose command he must depend, and to whose laws he must submit.[5]

The issue then in the Tree of Knowledge of Good and Evil was whether Adam would choose to decide for himself what is good and what is evil or whether he would accept what God had told him was good and evil.

The meaning of Adam's test concerning the Tree of Knowledge of Good and Evil becomes all the clearer if we consider how the serpent tempted Eve about it: "But the serpent said to the woman, 'You will not surely die. For God knows that when you eat of it your eyes will be opened, and you will be like God, knowing good and evil' " (Genesis 3:4–5). Notice how the serpent focused not on tree itself but on what God had said. The serpent undermined God's instructions rather than pointing to anything specific about the tree. Even the temptation locks attention on obeying God or choosing to go your own way.[6] The tree then did not *simply* examine whether Adam could properly discern good and evil, although that was involved. Rather, it crystalized the covenant demand to obey God in a very simple command, testing whether

Adam would listen to God or the devil. Some interpreters reject that Adam's ordeal with the tree and the serpent was a probation.[7] The better interpreters recognize that Adam faced a crisis moment that would decisively determine the future of his relationship with God, all concentrated in this trial of his obedience concerning a tree God had appointed with a special law, which is best described as probation.[8]

This tree was a trial of Adam's obedience, a probation testing his commitment to obey God in all things, yet our focus needs to remain on God's goodness in offering unimaginably great reward on the other side of that basic test. As already noted from Genesis 3:22, if Adam ate the Tree of Life, he would have lived forever. The Tree of Knowledge was the turning point of Adam's trial of obedience by which he could obtain unbreakable, everlasting communion with God.

In the New Testament, the apostle Paul infallibly interprets this creation narrative, confirming Adam's reward of deepened communion with God by describing the kind of life Adam could have obtained by his obedience. While describing the glories of the resurrection body, he explains:

> So is it with the resurrection of the dead. What is sown is perishable; what is raised is imperishable. It is sown in dishonor; it is raised in glory. It is sown in weakness; it is raised in power. It is sown a natural body; it is raised a spiritual body. If there is a natural body, there is also a spiritual body. Thus it is written, "The first man Adam became a living being"; the last Adam became a life-giving spirit. But it is not the spiritual that is first but the natural, and then the spiritual. The first man was from the earth, a man of dust; the second man is from heaven. As was the

> man of dust, so also are those who are of the dust, and as is the man of heaven, so also are those who are of heaven. Just as we have borne the image of the man of dust, we shall also bear the image of the man of heaven. (1 Corinthians 15:42–49)

Paul's description of our resurrection bodies focuses on their imperishable, glorified, and spiritual nature but relates fully to our understanding of God's covenant with Adam. After all, he cites Scripture to appeal to Adam's original state: "The first man Adam became a living creature (Genesis 2:7). Adam himself had a first condition of a perishable body, not that he would have naturally died since people did not die before the fall, but that he could die *if he sinned*. In this potential sense, Adam's first state was vulnerable.

Despite this perishable condition, Adam also had the prospect of an incorruptible, glorified, spiritual body. Paul writes in connection to his citation of the creation account, "If there is a natural body, there is also a spiritual body" (verse 44). Adam had the natural body by which he could disobey but could have obtained that incorruptible body. This spiritual body, far from being spiritual in the sense of disembodied or lacking physicality, was spiritual in relation to the Holy Spirit, who would bless Adam with a glorified, incorruptible body to confirm him in everlasting communion with God.[9] Adam's trial tested whether he would effectively and pointedly reflect the image of God by obeying his Maker in all things, particularly in choosing the right tree from which to eat, holding out the possibility of even deeper communion with God.

THE TRIUMPH

The troubling aspect of our reflections is that we know that Adam failed in his test. Despite being made upright in knowledge, righteousness, and holiness so that he was fully able to be and remain good, Adam chose the forbidden tree and threw us all into sin. His choice as our first representative put us all under the curse tied to the first tree. That can leave us feeling some despair. *We* are left under a curse because Adam represented us and took us to the wrong tree. God cast Adam and Eve from the garden, leaving us all blocked from the Tree of Life.

Too often, Christians, even if they know better, feel that our solution is to revert to that original covenant arrangement by trying to do our best to earn God's love through our works. There is a difference between striving hard after faithfulness to God out of gratitude for our salvation and feeling like we need to work our way into God's love. Even genuine Christians have this impulse to put ourselves back in Adam's shoes and try to earn blessings from God. We seem to think that if we try hard enough, if we push ourselves to be kind enough, love people enough, read our Bibles frequently, feed the homeless, and go to church, then God will love us and welcome us into his presence because of that.

The gospel is a far better solution. Even Adam in his original integrity was not committed enough to serve God well enough regarding a humble piece of fruit to earn blessings from God. Do we really think that we who suffer from the corruption of sin can perform the whole law well enough to punch our way past the gates of heaven?

After all, Adam already had God's love and favor in his original state of perfect righteousness, even if he was capable of earning higher blessings, but we stand under condemnation. We start on bad terms with God, rebels against his holiness and enemies of his kingdom. We are the children who did not clean our room quickly or slowly but tossed more rubbish around the whole house. We are the students who had everything we needed to pass the exam but tore it into pieces in front of the teacher and spit in his face. We cannot, therefore, depend on our works and our goodness to establish our blessings before God. We must not try to clean ourselves before God but must find a path to have our sins removed from us.

The triumph over Adam's failure is in Christ's victory, providing our hope for restoration to communion with God. Just as Adam closed the way to everlasting life by a tree, so Christ has opened it by a tree. Just as Adam gave himself to a tree and brought the curse, so Christ gave himself to a tree and removed the curse. Paul explains, "Christ redeemed us from the curse of the law by becoming a curse for us—for it is written, 'Cursed is everyone who is hanged on a tree'" (Galatians 3:13). Paul quotes Deuteronomy 21:23 that everyone who hangs on a tree is cursed to show how Christ bore our curse as he went to the cross. He bore our curse in his body so that by his wounds we would be healed.

Christ not only removes the curse of the Tree of Knowledge from us but also brings us all the way to the Tree of Life, that sacrament of everlasting, unbreakable communion with God. The developing narrative of Scripture shows how God frequently used trees to point us to the joyous communion that we have with him in Christ. When God instructed Israel how to build the tabernacle, the lampstand was a key feature of the Holy of Holies—the place of God's direct presence (Exodus 25:31–35). Notably, this lamp was to have six *branches*, each having a cup "made like almond blossoms," clearly shaping this marker of God's presence like a tree, harkening back to the Tree of Life (Exodus 25:31–40).[10] G. K. Beale and Mitchell Kim explain:

> Just as the Holy Place contained the lampstand shaped like the tree of life and the bread of the presence to sustain the priests, so the Garden of Eden is

> the place of the tree of life (Gen 2:8–9) and provides food to sustain Adam (Gen 2:16). Just as the outer court of Israel's second temple provided a place for the nations to come, so the land and seas to be subdued by Adam outside the Garden are the nations of Cush and Assyria (Gen 2:13–14); though, of course, these lands were not yet populated with peoples.[11]

In many respects, the temple renews the garden of Eden's imagery depicting God's provision for his people, even specifically concerning God's own presence, and notably does so by connecting the temple's lamp with the Tree of Life.[12]

The prophet Ezekiel further links trees to God's presence, specifically by associating trees with the temple, even giving them redemptive symbolism. Ezekiel begins his vision of the temple: "Then he brought me back to the door of the temple, and behold, water was issuing from below the threshold of the temple toward the east (for the temple faced east)" (Ezekiel 47:1). Multiple features already link the temple to the garden in Eden. First, water is prevalent, just like the four rivers surrounding Eden. Second, the water flowed eastward from the temple, emphasized repeatedly throughout this prophecy (Ezekiel 47:1–23). In contrast to how the waters that mark the place of God's presence are freely flowing eastward in this prophecy, as God exiled Adam and Eve from the garden, he blocked the *east* side to guard the Tree of Life: "He drove out the man, and at the east of the garden of Eden he placed the cherubim and a flaming sword that turned every way to guard the way to the tree of life" (Genesis 3:24).

Climatically, Ezekiel ties these other Edenic features directly to tree imagery. When Ezekiel was shown the eastern-flowing waters, he says, "As I went back, I saw on the bank of the river very many trees on the one side and on the other" (47:7) As he watched the waters flow east, bringing new life wherever it went, he noted its greater connection to trees:

> And on the banks, on both sides of the river, there will grow all kinds of trees for food. Their leaves will not wither, nor their fruit fail, but they will bear fresh fruit every month, because the water for them flows from the sanctuary. Their fruit will be for food, and their leaves for healing. (47:12)

Crucially, these trees relate to the water's life-giving effects as they too provide redemptive blessings. Indeed, their leaves provide healing.

This biblical theme of trees signifying everlasting life in communion with God climaxes in Christ as he brings us into the new creation. As the tree-shaped lampstand marked God's presence in the temple, so the church is two olive trees and two lampstands as we await Christ's coming (Revelation 11:4).[13] Jesus himself promises his people that "To the one who conquers I will grant to eat of the tree of life, which is in the paradise of God" (Revelation 2:7).

As Ezekiel was shown the watery temple accompanied by life-giving trees, so the apostle John glimpses the new creation as full of life-giving water and the Tree of Life itself:

> Then the angel showed me the river of the water of life, bright as crystal, flowing from the throne of God and of the Lamb through the middle of the street of the city; also, on either side of the river, the tree of life with its twelve kinds of fruit, yielding its fruit each month. The leaves of the tree were for the healing of the nations. (Revelation 22:1–2)

Most notably, the Tree of Life's leaves provided healing to the nations, just as the leaves Ezekiel saw. These new creation leaves also explicitly connect to God's presence as they grow next to this river of life that flows from the divine throne itself.

Christ is the source of this amazing divine provision, as he claimed the triumph where Adam failed. Adam's work blocked our way to the Tree of Life (Genesis 3:22), but Christ grants its fruit to us by his grace. John explains, "Blessed are those who wash their robes, so that they may have *the right to the tree of life* and that they may enter the city by the gates " (Revelation 22:14). Adam failed to obtain the right to eat from the Tree of Life, resulting in exile from the garden. As the last Adam, Jesus Christ has earned the right to eat from the tree but passes its fruit to his people. He gives this access to those whose robes are washed, namely those whose sins have been forgiven by his own blood. So, let us wash our robes by running to the Lord Jesus so that he might clothe us with his righteousness and provide us a full portion of fruit from the Tree of Life, healing us unto everlasting communion with God.

CONCLUSION

Good teachers examine their students not to prove them stupid but to showcase their abilities. God tested Adam in the garden in Eden not to prove him unworthy but as an opportunity to display the goodness of the creature whom he had made with knowledge, righteousness, and holiness. Adam had all that he needed to pass his probation but chose to fail, believing the liar rather than the Lord. Mercifully, God is a uniquely good and benevolent teacher, so rather than failing all whom Adam represented, he sent Christ to retake the exam for us, letting us gain from the reward of the Savior. By faith, we are switched from Adam's representation to Christ's and so, being clothed in his righteousness, gain access to the Tree of Life and enter into incorruptible, everlasting communion with God.

QUESTIONS FOR FURTHER REFLECTION

1. With all the trees that God had given for food to Adam and Eve, why did he forbid them to eat of the tree of the knowledge of good and evil?

2. Signs are used to signify and seal the promises and curses of a covenant. How does the Tree of Life function as a sacramental sign of the covenant God had with Adam?

3. How does the biblical theme of trees carry forward from creation to the fall to the Mosaic temple to Christ's redemptive work to the new heavens and the new earth?

4. Even now, how do we default to Adam's original test of trying to earn God's favor? Why are we not qualified to even sit for that exam? How did the second Adam claim victory for us?

CREATURELY COMMUNION

Designed for Togetherness

God's covenant with Adam showed how he intended us to have blessed communion with him from the outset. Even apart from the Fall, people would have more relationships than just a direct connection to God. We would also relate to one another. How does this feature of our human life relate to our communion with God?

Christians have always thought about how they might find an illustration in creation to help explain the Trinity, regardless of how well those endeavors turned out. In the church's ancient period, theologians asked a question about whether creation contains what they called *vestiges of the Trinity*. Although they readily denied that we can ever fully understand God and that nature could ever provide an illustration that perfectly captured the reality of the Lord, they still sought for ways that nature corresponded to the truth of who God is. Hilary of Poitier wrote in the fourth century:

> The slowness and difficulty whereby our human nature grasps divine things makes it necessary to remind ourselves frequently of what we have formerly stressed, that we should not look upon human analogies as completely satisfactory in explaining the mysteries of the divine power, but that the illustrations of an earthly nature are only employed in order to direct our mind in a spiritual way to heavenly things, in order that we may move forward along this step of our nature to the comprehension of the divine majesty.[1]

Although creation cannot teach the fullness of truth about God, Hilary argued that earthly things can guide our minds in limited ways to understand the divine majesty.

Despite the question being common, not all entirely agreed about it. In contrast with Hilary, Gregory of Nazianzus, also writing in the fourth century, concluded: "I have very carefully considered this matter in my own mind, and have looked at it in every point of view, in order to find some illustration of this most important subject, but I have been unable to discover anything on earth with which to compare the nature of the Godhead."[2] On the other hand, Augustine, arguably the foremost fourth-century theologian, argued:

> When therefore we regard the Creator, who is understood by the things that are made we must understand the Trinity of whom there appear traces in the creature, as is fitting. For in that Trinity is the supreme source of all things, and the most perfect beauty, and the most blessed delight.[3]

His point was that since God is the source of all creatures, namely as their Maker, they must bear even faint hints of their designer. No creature is identical to God, since that would undermine the Creator-creature distinction, but each does have some creaturely fitting way of reflecting the splendor of the God who made them. Augustine said that even traces of the Trinity appear in the creature, particularly us.

This question about vestiges of the Trinity really concerns how much we can know about God from what we call *general revelation*. On the one hand, *special revelation* is what God makes known to us in direct ways by speaking overtly in human language, for example, prophecy, visions, and, most pointedly and still today, in the inspired and written Scripture. On the other hand, in *general revelation,* God grants true but limited understanding of who he is through features of creation.[4] The apostle Paul explains this point in Romans 1:19–20: "For what can be known about God is plain to them, because God has shown it to them. For *his invisible attributes*, namely, his eternal power and divine nature, have been clearly perceived, ever since the creation of the world, *in the things that have been made*. So they are without excuse." In other words, creation naturally and generally reveals truths concerning God. Although sinners reject and suppress these truths that nature makes known, creation does continually reveal them, some being engraved upon our very hearts (Romans 1:18, 32; 2:14–15). Concerning vestiges of the Trinity, some theologians have wondered if nature spoke not just about God's general attributes but also about God as Trinity.[5]

Since God is so splendidly majestic, it seems unlikely that his *triune* glory could fail to shine into creation in *some* way. Augustine was convinced that man must reveal God's triunity in some way, since we are made in the image of the *triune* God:

> For it was not that gods might make, or make after the image and likeness of gods; but that the Father, and Son, and Holy Spirit might make after the image of the Father, and Son, and Holy Spirit, that man might subsist as the image of God. And God is the Trinity. But because that image of God was not made altogether equal to Him, as being not born of Him, but created by Him; in order to signify this, he is in such way the image as that he is "after the image," that is, he is not made equal by parity, but approaches to Him by a sort of likeness.[6]

Although Augustine's principle is straightforward enough, John Calvin rightly chastises him for applying it too imaginatively: "But Augustine, beyond all others, speculates with excessive refinement, for the purpose of fabricating a Trinity in man. For in laying hold of the three faculties enumerated by Aristotle, the intellect, the memory, and the will, he afterwards out of one Trinity derives many."[7] Calvin highlights how finding a threefold makeup of our distinct human faculties is far too creative and this sort of threefold pattern does not allow us to understand the Trinity from natural revelation. Despite some creative attempts to prove the doctrine of the Trinity from aspects of creation, especially our human nature, we ultimately need God to explain to us in special revelation that he is Father, Son, and Spirit. We cannot know that truth unless God *tells* it to us.[8]

Although nothing in nature allows us to learn that God is triune by reason alone, perhaps we should not abandon the entire premise, looking rather for something about creation that fittingly *reflects* that God is triune.[9] Certainly, we depend on Scripture to know that the true God is Father, Son, and Spirit. Still, God's image bearers may have *some sort* of imprint of God's triune nature, not in a speculative threefold pattern but in something more general about our constitution or even our commission. In this respect, Thomas Aquinas helps us strike a balance. For, on the one hand, he argues that we need special revelation to know about the Trinity:

> It is impossible to attain to the knowledge of the Trinity by natural reason ... Therefore, by natural reason we can know what belongs to the unity of the essence, but not what belongs to the distinction of the persons. Whoever, then, tries to prove the trinity of persons by natural reason derogate from faith [citing Hebrews 11:1 and 1 Corinthians 2:6–7].[10]

On the other hand, he also notes how *traces* provide clues that help us to recognize the correspondence between causes and their effects, much like smoke is not fire but nonetheless, as a *trace*, fittingly represents that fire is or had been present. In relation to God:

> But in all creatures there is found the trace of the Trinity, inasmuch as in every creature are found some things which are necessarily reduced to the divine Persons as to their cause. For every creature subsists in its own being, and has a form, whereby it is determined to be a species, and has relation to something else.[11]

Like how we may not know what our birthday present is until we unwrap it but in hindsight recognize all the signs and clues that fittingly hinted at this gift, so too we need God to tell us that he is triune but his triunity makes perfect sense when we recognize some of the fitting indicators built into creation, especially regarding the way that we are made in his image.[12] The question is, if Calvin rightly restrained Augustine's too speculative application of a good principle in regard to finding threefold patterns in human nature, what is a responsible way to see vestiges of the Trinity in God's image bearers?

Genesis' narrative concerning our creation helps us find the answer: Just as our God can but dwell only in eternal loving communion as the Father, Son, and Spirit, so too should those creatures who bear his image be marked by communion among ourselves. After God created Adam, he looked upon him and observed that it was not good that man was alone (Genesis 2:18). Our need for fellowship does not make God's triune nature known to us, properly speaking, but is certainly a fitting mark upon the creatures who represent the God who eternally dwells in Trinitarian communion.[13] When God made the woman so that Adam would not be alone, it pinpointed how the God who is eternally in communion as Father, Son, and Spirit should be represented by a creature who also has a fitting partner for communion on the creaturely plane. So then, God created man, male and female, in his own image, fit for communion with him, but also needing creaturely communion together as a reverberation of our triune God who exists in eternal communion. This chapter explores the main point that God's image best reflects God as we live and work in communion.

OUR COMMISSION

When God created man, male and female, he constituted us for a specific relationship with him and to creation, and this relationality is built into our commission to reflect the divine image. As we noted when looking at God's creation of the garden in Eden as a place for communion, Genesis 2:4–25 rewinds the creation story to zoom in on and expand on the events recorded as the sixth day in Genesis 1:24–31, using much greater detail concerning the creation of humanity.[14] In the first, more general account of man's creation, God summarized humanity's duties as the divine image bearer by saying, "Be fruitful and multiply and fill the earth and subdue it, and have dominion over the fish of the sea and over the birds of the heavens and over every living thing that moves on the earth" (Genesis 1:28). Adam and Eve were to continue God's work of filling the earth and reigning over the other creatures that do not bear God's image but to do so after a creaturely fashion. In Genesis 2:18–25, God provides more detail on how we should go about these creaturely commissions.

There are two crucial aspects, one more obvious than the other, to consider concerning that creaturely commission in this account of how God created humanity, male and female, in his image. First, more specifically, God created man and woman to be husband and wife, making this passage naturally important for how we understand God's purposes for marriage. Marriage, however, does not exhaust this passage's relevance concerning human relationships and our responsibility to bear God's image. Second and more generally, this passage teaches that all people, made after God's likeness, need to be in communion with other people. By our very constitution, we need friendship, fellowship, and love. Since both those specific and general teachings are important lessons to take from this text, neither to be shorted in what they might teach us about the Lord and living faithfully for him, the next chapter explores Genesis' teaching about marriage, but this chapter reflects more deeply on that more general teaching about our essential need for relationships with one another.

Fundamentally, Adam needed communion with at least one other creature who was fit for fellowship with him, a need we share because that need marks humanity's existence as God's image. We are made to reflect the true God who exists eternally in the communion of Father, Son, and Spirit.[15] God inherently has relationships within himself, since the Father, Son, and Spirit exist as eternal relations within the Godhead. As the Athanasian Creed teaches,

> And the catholic faith is this: That we worship one God in Trinity, and Trinity in Unity; neither confounding the Persons, nor dividing the Essence. For there is one Person of the Father: another of the Son: and another of the Holy Ghost. But the Godhead of the Father, of the Son, and of the Holy Ghost, is all one; the Glory equal, the Majesty coeternal.[16]

So, we are made in the image and likeness of the God who exists in eternal relationships.

Because we are the bearers of God's image, our need for communion makes us an analogy, even if a "faint analogy," to the God who is the communion of Father, Son, and Spirit.[17] An analogy draws a relationship between two things that are not identical but correspond. Famously, Forrest Gump said, "Life is like a box of chocolates; you never know what you're going to get." Life is not a box of chocolates, as if our existence consists of a mixture of cocoa, milk, and sugar. Rather, there is a relationship between how life plays out and the way that we experience a box of chocolates. With a box of chocolates, you cannot see through the chocolate coating to know what specific flavor each piece contains, making it an endeavor of surprises to eat these candies. *In this respect*, life resembles a box of chocolates in that it too is full of unexpected things.

Concerning our relationship to God as his image bearers, we are not identical to God but are like him in some ways appropriate to creatures. For example, God is Father, and I am a father. These words are the same, but their meaning is not exactly identical. Still, the meaning is related in that creaturely fatherhood is enabled by and reflects in a creaturely way God's Fatherhood. The meanings are *analogical*. This analogous relationship underscores our reflections from chapter two regarding the Creator-creature distinction. Nevertheless, although never in a way that undermines that distinction, our relationship to God as his image bearers demands that we have some resemblance to him. For example, God is holy and righteous in an absolute and transcendent way, yet we have his moral law, a summary description of his own character, stamped on our hearts as those made in his likeness. More specific for our reflection here, God dwells in eternal communion as the Trinity, and therefore, we live in need of communion.[18]

God's manner of creating us makes this connection clear. As Genesis 1:26–27 narrates, when God created humanity in his image, he conferred with himself about his creative work:

> Then God said, "Let us make man in our image, after our likeness. And let them have dominion over the fish of the sea and over the birds of the heavens and over the livestock and over all the earth and over every creeping thing that creeps on the earth."

God's self-deliberation of "Let *us* make man in *our* own image" is most likely the first recorded instance of a conversation within the Trinity.[19]

The church's historical interpretation of this verse attests to this view's persuasiveness. As far back as the second century, Irenaeus argued, "And God said, Let us make man after our image and likeness. For there is seen in this place the Father speaking to the Son, the Wonderful Counselor of the Father."[20] In Belgic

Confession article 9, Reformed churches formally receive this interpretation as their own:

> The testimonies of the Holy Scriptures that teach us to believe this Holy Trinity are written in many places of the Old Testament, which are not so necessary to enumerate as to choose them out with discretion and judgment. In Genesis 1:26, 27, God says: *Let us make man in our image, after our likeness, etc. So God created man in His own image, male and female created He them.* And Genesis 3:22: *Behold, the man is become as one of us.* From this saying, *Let us make man in our image*, it appears that there are more persons than one in the Godhead; and when He says *God created*, He signifies the unity. It is true He does not say how many persons there are, but that which appears to us somewhat obscure in the Old Testament is very plain in the New.[21]

Christians have then long seen God's self-address as revealing the Trinity.

God's self-deliberation marks the creation account in pivotal and prominent ways. Throughout the various works of creation, God speaks directly to creation but self-deliberates only when fashioning the creatures who bear his image. In contrast to the *impersonal* decrees concerning the other facets of creation, the Scripture records God's intratrinitarian consultation in connection to humanity because we are marked with God's *personal* concern.[22] When commanding light to exist, the waters to separate, the land to gather, and the earth to bring forth its fruits, God never reflected about the matter. As he came to form man in his likeness, however, he conferred about this creature, setting this creative work apart as special within the narrative and highlighting our place within the world.[23]

Pastorally, this point reminds us of humanity's unique and intrinsic value. God has set his image upon *us*, marking us special among the creatures. This value grounds why we are to treat one another well, striving to live at peace with all men, so much as our part makes that possible (Romans 12:18). We are to value one another, not fighting, abusing, or using our fellow humans. We were meant for more.

In that respect, our creation after God's likeness also marks our need for fellowship at the creaturely level. Just as Genesis 1:26–27 narrates that God conferred with himself before creating us, so too, Genesis 2:18 again tells how the triune God self-deliberated, again in relation to creating his image bearers: "It is not good that the man should be alone; I will make him a helper fit for him." Continuing the intratrinitarian consultation, between creating Adam and creating the woman, God observed that it was not good that the man should be alone—the only time in the creation story that God does not declare that what he has made is good as it is. The man needs companionship. The insights from Genesis 1:26–27 and 2:18 both highlight God's internal conversation. So, as God forged his image bearers, he marked those born out of the Trinitarian conversation with a need for communion. Our constitution as God's image bearers entails our commission, our responsibility, that we live and work together in creaturely communion with one another so that we properly reflect and represent the God whose image we reflect.

OUR COMMITMENT

So far, we have established a theological point that since God is eternally Father, Son, and Spirit in communion, it is fitting that his image bearers would have communion at the creaturely level.

Humanity belongs together since God made us with a specific intent that we would not be alone. That premise has significant bearing on how we live before God, prompting us to reflect on how that theological foundation shapes our commitments to one another.

As we saw concerning Genesis 2:5–7 that the land's lack of rain introduced a dilemma for God to solve, so too the observation that man should not be alone signals another point of tension in the developing narrative. Moreover, that tension heightens as Adam sets about his initial tasks, not knowing that God would soon make a wife for him. God himself had declared the dilemma by noting that man should not be alone. The next step of the story is striking:

> Now out of the ground the LORD God had formed every beast of the field and every bird of the heavens and brought them to the man to see what he would call them. And whatever the man called every living creature, that was its name. The man gave names to all livestock and to the birds of the heavens and to every beast of the field. But for Adam there was not found a helper fit for him. (Genesis 2:19–20)

By inserting Adam's interaction with the animals directly after the observation that man should not be alone, the narrative signals that Adam's relationship with them is an initial foray into overcoming this issue of isolation. The result, however, was that as he went about naming the animals, Adam began to realize—as have the attentive readers—that none of them was truly fitting to provide him with proper creaturely communion.[24]

The connection between Adam's need for companionship and its realization as he set about his image-bearing task of exercising dominion over the other creatures indicates that the deficiency of Adam's isolation was not simply or directly about his loneliness. After all, Adam had the significant task of being the priest of the garden-temple who was meant to fill the earth but could not accomplish that task alone.[25] So God made Eve to help him in that priestly task, showing how God's people *as a whole* function as a royal priesthood within the world, as the apostle Peter said is still true of the church holistically today: "But you are a chosen race, a royal priesthood, a holy nation, a people for his own possession, that you may proclaim the excellencies of him who called you out of darkness into his marvelous light" (1 Peter 2:9).[26] Regardless, Adam needed a fitting partner to work alongside him so that he might fulfill his vocation as God's image.

These reflections teach us an important lesson, namely, that we cannot accomplish what God calls us to do in this world on our own. Nor are we meant to, since that is not how we are designed. All the same, sometimes we try to live as though we should achieve all things on our own. It is a terrible human tendency that in times of distress and trial, we distance and isolate ourselves from others. But it never goes well for us to be apart. Think about the tower of Babel and those who tried to build it for their own glory: God cursed them by separating and dividing them (Genesis 11:1–9). Separation and division are then a curse.

Writing this book at the start of 2022 as the lingering effects of 2020's COVID-19 pandemic persist among us, I cannot help but think about how the previous two years have made this theological point that separation and division curse us into a practical and felt reality. In the United Kingdom, especially for the in some ways overpopulated city of London—where I was a pastor—which lacks personal space and room to wander easily outside, people were locked inside their homes for months on end. Over the duration of the most intense seasons of our lockdown, the most critical pastoral issue that rose quickly to the fore was that of collapsing mental health. Isolated people went into tailspins of depression and overthinking. Even while constantly reaching out to speak to others as their pastor, I still felt the increasing toll that separation from others was taking on my mental well-being. In God's providence, even the direst cases have improved since then. Nonetheless, we should not let ourselves quickly forget the genuine damage that people endure by being cut off from fellowship with others. Nor should we pretend that these cases are limited to times of national crisis or that the causes of people's horrible experiences in this way are limited to externally imposed lockdowns. Many of God's people suffer every day with overwhelming loneliness and isolation, whether due to objective or subjective trials. As much as lies within us, this should not be.

That problem has drastic ramifications for the life of Christ's church. Our existence as the kingdom of priests bearing God's name into the world harkens back to that creation principle of God's people working together. In that respect, Paul's argument that we are the body of Christ takes on new significance in how it illustrates that we cannot properly function as the church without one another:

> For just as the body is one and has many members, and all the members of the body, though many, are one body, so it is with Christ. For in one Spirit we were all baptized into one body—Jews or Greeks, slaves or free—and all were made to drink of one Spirit. For the body does not consist of one member but of many ... The eye cannot say to the hand, "I have no need of you," nor again the head to the feet, "I have no need of you." On the contrary, the parts of the body that seem to be weaker are indispensable,

> and on those parts of the body that we think less honorable we bestow the greater honor, and our unpresentable parts are treated with greater modesty, which our more presentable parts do not require. But God has so composed the body, giving greater honor to the part that lacked it, that there may be no division in the body, but that the members may have the same care for one another. If one member suffers, all suffer together; if one member is honored, all rejoice together. Now you are the body of Christ and individually members of it. (1 Corinthians 12:12–14, 21–27)

This creation principle that has renewed grounds in Christ calls us to consider our life together. The church must be a people who look not to our own interests but also to the interests of others (Philippians 2:4). Very pointedly, that requires that we give our fellowship to one another. No matter how extroverted or introverted we are and even regardless of how much you like or dislike the people in your church—remembering that you in your sin give them just as much reason to dislike you as they give you—we must be committed to communion with one another.

Our commitment cannot be only communal nor limited only to how we treat others when *they* feel isolated or alone for objective or subjective reasons. We all have a tendency, when we are fearful of the world or the future or our situation, to retreat into solitude. We react to troubles by thinking that being alone will help us avoid our difficulties. We develop reasons why we should be alone, why we should not seek fellowship with others, or why no one wants fellowship with us. Often, we then grow angry and bitter with one another, becoming ever more critical. It is no coincidence that the most internally united congregations are those where people know how to engage in genuine fellowship. In all circumstances, our sin easily facilitates that we grow increasingly divided and separated, which is a curse. So, our commitment must be to have communion together as God's people.

OUR COMMUNION

President John F. Kennedy famously said, "Ask not what your country can do for you, but what you can do for your country." As we think about how to work out our commitment as the church to have communion together more practically, we must acknowledge that we all too readily think of all the ways that we want our church family to serve us, locking our focus on what we wish others would do for our good. The irony is that we often find ourselves most satisfied from serving someone else. This irony should not surprise us, though, because Paul reminds us that Jesus said, "It is more blessed to give than to receive" (Acts 20:35). We need to reflect on what it looks like to live life together as the people of God.

Unfortunately, although theologians have often tried to commandeer the doctrine of the Trinity to support various social agendas, leaving us leery of applying Trinitarian theology to our ethical principles, our reflections here support that there are some basic ways in which our understanding of the triune God should shape our practice. You, Christian, must live your life in communion with the church in an others-centered way because that reflects God's own character. God's Triune communion is extrospective, with each person fully delighting in the glory of the others from all eternity as the Father, Son, and Spirit pulse with immutable love for one another. Even in the economy of redemption, Christ's actions and prayers reveal how the Father glorifies the Son, the Son glorifies the Father, and the Spirit glorifies both, marking the Trinitarian communion as others centered. Although applications could quickly be pressed too far and too tenuously, the principle is that this Trinitarian shape of communion is built inherently into our constitution as God's image bearers.[27]

There are two things that we can *do* in this light. First, we need to make the effort to reach out to others in our church more often. This effort does not need to be special or extravagantly organized. We just need to pick up the phone and stay in contact more, perhaps inviting people to stop by more often. The fact that you may not feel like you need more or deeper fellowship is far from the point because you are not the focus here. You may not need someone else's fellowship, but someone else might need yours. Sometimes those people are not the ones who first come to mind, which is exactly why we need to spread ourselves more widely, although not overstretching ourselves, in reaching out to more people in our church for fellowship. Contact maintains communion.

Second, because division is a curse, we need to work hard not to be critical or derisive. Churches easily develop cliques and subgroups, often fostered out of complaints about various features of church life. But that negativity feeds the curse of Babel. If you have an issue, go to someone directly rather than complaining to a third party. Go in hopes of clarification and reconciliation. Go repentantly and humbly, and work for the betterment of everyone. Do not complain but build better relationships to foster further communion. Redirect your efforts to contributing rather than complaining so that improvement occurs.

The reason we must be so mindful of our commitment and its applications is that sin has fractured and still fractures our communion. Our communion has a vertical and a horizontal dimension, but sin damages both. Sin, as rebellion against God and his law, has put us at enmity with our Maker and destroys the communion between Creator and creature. Sin fractures our vertical communion with God by making us his enemies. Further, sin, by how it corrupts our nature, fractures our horizontal communion with one another and destroys our creaturely communion. We become self-centered and hostile, which is why nations have wars, why friends gossip about each other, why kids are disobedient, and why we make a mess of so many of our relationships. We have broken our relationship with God and so unwound our communion with the Creator, and then we attack one another.

Alienation and separation run rampant in the wake of sin as the enemies of fellowship and communion. Adam and Eve's alienation from one another becomes apparent as, even though they once were naked and unashamed together, they cover their nakedness in guilty shame after they sinned (Genesis 3:7).[28] The alienation between humanity and God becomes apparent as, just like they hid their bodies from one another, they hide their whole selves from the God who made them as he enters the garden (Genesis 3:8–10). The way that sinners turn outward in hostility as wickedness breaches communion becomes clear from the outset of sin, as Adam immediately blames his wife and blames God for giving him his wife, so demonstrating that communion with the Creator is broken and communion among creatures is damaged (Genesis 3:11–12). This break of communion both vertically and horizontally leaves us with a troubled plight still today.

Hence, Christ came not simply to save individuals but also to build a church. From its outset, the body of Christ joined together people who were previously separated:

> So then you are no longer strangers and aliens, but you are fellow citizens with the saints and members of the household of God, built on the foundation of the apostles and prophets, Christ Jesus himself being the cornerstone, in whom the whole structure, being

> joined together, grows into a holy temple in the Lord. In him you also are being built together into a dwelling place for God by the Spirit. (Ephesians 2:19–22)

The gospel then provides not only for the healing of our relationship with God but also for our restoration to fellowship with other people.

CONCLUSION

Just as, even before sin wreaked its havoc, Adam could not fix his own problem of estrangement from a fitting partner for fellowship by his works but had to rely on God to provide the solution, all the more after sin has afflicted us must we realize that we must rely on God to overcome our plight of alienation and separation. The solution to our plight in both its vertical and horizontal aspects is Christ. The gospel announces that "while we were still weak, at the right time Christ died for the ungodly ... but God shows his love for us in that while we were still sinners, Christ died for us ... For if while we were enemies we were reconciled to God by the death of his Son, much more, now that we are reconciled, shall we be saved by his life" (Romans 5:6, 8, 10–11). Sin results in a death sentence, separating us from the God who is himself abundant life. Christ died precisely to bear your curse of separation from God. He endured all the divine wrath that was due for your sin, so that God's enemies would become God's friends by faith. We are reconciled to communion with God in Christ.

That reconciliation extends to the horizontal dimension that is our creaturely communion as well. In his high priestly prayer, Christ, on the basis of his saving work, prayed, "Holy Father, keep them in your name, which you have given me, that they may be one, even as we are one ... I do not ask for these only, but also for those who will believe in me through their word, that they may all be one, just as you, Father, are in me, and I in you, that they also may be in us, so that the world may believe that you have sent me" (John 17:11, 20–21). Christ by his mission of salvation has purchased a people for himself, whom the Father binds *together* in communion both with God and one another.

QUESTIONS FOR FURTHER REFLECTION

1. How do we as creatures living and working in communion reflect, in part, aspects of the Trinity?
2. How does God's self-deliberation upon the creation of man distinguish man from the other creatures? What implications does this reality have on the value of all human life?
3. What did Adam learn in naming the animals?
4. Given this chapter's point that the economy of redemption shows the Trinitarian persons glorifying each other, how does this doctrine of the Trinity dictate how we are to commune with others within the church? Give practical examples.
5. How does sin distort a proper view of communion with others?

COMMUNION POINTING TO CHRIST

Marriage

Marriage evokes many different ideas for various people. Some first think of the wedding ceremony and the day of celebration. Others immediately imagine buying a house and a minivan and settling down. Still others may think of old age and walks along the beach with their spouse in the golden years. Regardless of what ideas it may first conjure for you, marriage is at rock bottom about communion. It is God's appointed institution for joining two people's lives together in the most intimate link between creatures.

Our previous study reflected on how God's Trinitarian communion reverberated into creation as he made humanity in his image, forging them with a fitting need for creaturely communion. God's intratrinitarian conversation about creating his image brought forth his image bearers, who were not good on their own but needed to be male and female as fitting partners for fellowship to carry God's likeness into the world. God's creation of humanity in his image has that general aspect that we need to be in creaturely communion together as those who represent the God who eternally dwells in inherent communion.

On top of that more general aspect of a need for creaturely communion built into us as God's image, marriage adds another more specific aspect of our need for communion. In Genesis 2:18–25, Scripture highlights how God designed man and woman for marriage to address the need that man should not be alone. This chapter explores the main point that marriage is meant for communion and points us to the communion we have with God in Christ.

PORTRAYING COMMUNION

Although the creation narrative entails many fundamental truths about marriage, our reflections here focus on establishing that God appointed marriage primarily to address the issue of creaturely communion. As we saw in chapter eight, God's command to Adam in Genesis 2:15–17 was a covenant offering incorruptible life to Adam for his obedience. Following directly on making that covenant with Adam, God observed, "It is not good that the man should be alone; I will make him a helper fit for him" (Genesis 2:18). The narrative's pace closely relates to Adam's covenant and his need for a wife. Just as God had entered communion by covenant with Adam, so too he would create a partner for creaturely communion with Adam fit for the covenant of marriage.

Strikingly, although it was not good for Adam to be alone, he was not alone in an absolute sense. Remember, God had previously made the animals prior to creating Adam: "Now, the Lord God had already formed from the ground all the animals of the field and all the birds of the skies but now made them come to Adam to see what he would name them, and so whatever the man named a living creature was its name" (Genesis 2:19).[1] Not accidentally, God observed that it is not good for man to be alone and then directly afterward brought the animals to him. The narrative builds suspense as we watch Adam learn that none of the existing animals were suitable as his partner, making the point to Adam and to us that he needed a fitting helper who did not yet exist.[2] The end of Adam's first task marks that discovery: "The man gave names to all livestock and to the birds of the heavens and to every beast of the field. But for Adam there was *not found a helper fit for him*" (Genesis 2:20). Although Adam had the animals for some sort of company, none of them were *fitting helpers* for him and therefore did not provide the creaturely communion he needed.

Adam's mission in creation helps us understand why the animals were not fit partners to help Adam, leaving him without proper creaturely communion. In Genesis 1:28, God declared that Adam was to "have dominion over the fish of the sea and over the birds of the heavens and over every living thing that moves on the earth." In the ancient Near East, the act of naming someone or something entailed authority over them or it. God had named parts of the whole creation—day and night, etc.—and remained the supreme ruler even as he brought the animals to Adam. Still, Adam imitated God and his authority, exercising his creaturely dominion by naming the animals.[3] We see how clearly the creation account indicates that God delegated his kingly authority to Adam, at least in a sense, as God, rather than naming the animals himself as he had done with other aspects of the created order, brought them to Adam, handing him some responsibility in this authoritative task. The problem was that as Adam had this sort of dominion authority over all these creatures, he had no proper helper for his task of bearing the divine image in covenant with God.[4]

Crucially, directly after God's act of explicitly stating his covenant with Adam by issuing the command about the tree of knowledge, he created the woman for Adam to have in the covenant of marriage. Hence, Adam rejoiced that he no longer looked for help among the animals but had found the bone of his bone and flesh of his flesh:

> "This at last is bone of my bones
> and flesh of my flesh;
> she shall be called Woman,
> because she was taken out of Man." (Genesis 2:23)

This woman, his co-image bearer, was the partner fit for communion with him in covenant.

The lesson we take away from this fast-paced narrative of God covenanting with Adam directly followed by making a creaturely partner to covenant with Adam in marriage is that the communion by covenant that God entered with man is to be mirrored in an intimate relationship between his image-bearing creatures as well. Thus, God formed the two sexes, male and female, to mirror the communion of God and his image. In the first place, God and humanity are fundamentally different, reminding us again of the Creator-creature distinction, yet humanity has a fitting likeness and correspondence to God so that we of all the creatures have the most intimate communion with God. In the second place, likewise, man and woman are also different. Being two fully distinct sexes yet have a fitting likeness and correspondence to one another, they can have the most intimate communion among creatures. The immutable difference between man and woman therefore reflects how humanity is different from God yet is meant for wonderful relationship with him. Marriage as the joining of two others—man and woman—is the fitting analogy of our relationship with God in that God and humanity are immutably and fundamentally different yet well fit for relationship.

In that respect as well, marriage between man and woman, joined as distinct sexes in one communion—so a union of others—models how God who is distinct and different from us makes communion with us. It is, therefore, vital to marriage that the parties be different from one another, else it is not properly illustrative of the communion with God it was meant to reflect. Everything about humanity was crafted for communion with God, and marriage was designed for portraying communion with God.

PRACTICING COMMUNION

So far, we have reflected on how God fashioned marriage between man and woman as the creaturely communion that portrays the communion that humanity was designed to have with God. That theological reality is visible and valuable to everyone, as proper and healthy marriage should portray vital communion as we can have with God. Even if you are not married (or not *yet* married), marriage remains a benefit for you by seeing these gospel-shaped relationships as a demonstration of the relationship that Christ has with you. This value prompts us to think more practically about what marriage as an analogy of our communion with God teaches us.

This general value of marriage informs us all about our sexual ethics. First, as Adam married Eve, "the man and his wife were both naked and were not ashamed" (Genesis 2:25). Nothing in the text demands that we, as the human race holistically, would never have made clothes if sin had not occurred. After all, we will be *clothed* in fine white robes in the new creation even after sin is totally removed from us (Revelation 7:9–14). The narrative already made clear that the seasons still changed in the pre-fall era, reminding us that we use clothes for warmth and protection from the elements, not just because of sinful shame, which well may have been a need as Adam ventured to the garden's borders as he worked to expand paradise across the globe. Rather, shameless nudity belonged by creation in the marital context. Either way, we know that *because of sin* Adam and Eve were ashamed even when only the two of them were present. Marriage, however, should be the specific context where we should not be ashamed of our sexuality.

This connection also substantiates why sex outside of marriage is sinful. We should think back to our discussion in chapter five about virtues and how we obey God's commands but also reflect on how God's moral commands correspond to deeper realities. Accordingly, our role as God's image bearers and God's bringing us forth from his intratrinitarian conversation ground the sinfulness of extramarital sex. To remind ourselves about some of the facets of this virtue outlook, the Ten Commandments—God's moral law—describe God's character. Regarding the issue at hand, the seventh commandment forbids adultery *because* God is faithful only to those with whom he has formal communion. God made communion not with badgers and bears but with Adam and Eve, his image bearers and covenant partners. He spoke only to them. After the fall, God grants his saving communion only to believers and not to those who do not belong to his people. Hence, the moral law calls us as God's image bearers to avoid extramarital sex because we, like God, grant the most intimate of communion only within our formal covenants, namely marriage.

God's manner in creating us further confirms our point. We considered in the previous chapter how the communion of God's intratrinitarian conversation—"Let us make man in our own image"—brought forth a creature fit for communion with him and for creaturely communion. God's self-deliberation within that most intimate intratrinitarian communion as he created humanity clarifies that the most intimate communion is the appropriate setting for reproduction. Our triune God confers communally about creating humanity in the divine image, signaling that communion and replication, specifically joined together, are marks of God's character. Communion is part of what it means to be God and so should also belong to what it means to be God's image.[5] God's image bearers, therefore, reproduce and use the sexual intimacy that results in reproduction only within the confines of special communion in marriage.

In addition to these general lessons for everyone, regardless of marital status, the account of Adam and Eve's marriage prompts important considerations directly for married people too. Most pointedly, if marriage is meant to portray the communion that we have with God, then are we conducting our marriages in a way that demonstrates lives of communion together? Sometimes we turn our marriages into contracts by which we get what we want from the relationship at the expense of the other person. As Christians, this is not how we should be in any relationship, especially marriage. We should not be negligent, absent, overbearing, or nagging. We should focus not on our own interests but on fermenting communion. We must be purposeful in the type of communion we develop in our marriages.

In this light, God formed the woman from the man's rib to be Adam's fitting partner in covenant.[6]

> So the Lord God caused a deep sleep to fall upon the man, and while he slept took one of his ribs and closed up its place with flesh. And the rib that the Lord God had taken from the man he made into a woman and brought her to the man. (Genesis 2:21–22)

Matthew Henry, the Puritan Bible commentator, famously noted, "Not made out of his head to top him, not out of his feet to be trampled upon by him, but out of his side to be equal with him, under his arm to be protected, and near his heart to be beloved."[7] The creation account is very specific in explaining how God created the woman to solve the problem that Adam needed a *helper*.

The woman's role as helper signifies how she would make an *essential and needed* contribution to the man's life. The point has nothing to do with any supposed inferiority or inadequacy of women in relation to men. Throughout the Old Testament, this Hebrew word for "helper" appears nineteen times, sixteen of those instances referring to God in relation us.[8] The New Testament then calls the Holy Spirit our Helper (John 14:16, 26). Certainly, we are not superior to God, nor is he our subordinate in any sense, so the woman's role as "helper" does not denote inferiority in her creation either. Although Scripture is clear that men are supposed to be the leaders in their households, that does not mean that every woman is supposed to submit to every man in society. Since God serving as our helper does not mean that God submits to us, so too then Scripture does not require that women as women submit to men in the general task of bearing God's image.

Adam's reaction upon meeting his wife moreover teaches us a lesson about the sort of communion we should foster in our marriages. As God brought the woman to him, Adam celebrated:

> "This at last is bone of my bones
>   and flesh of my flesh;
> she shall be called Woman,
>   because she was taken out of Man." (Genesis 2:23)

In the Hebrew text, as signaled by the unusual capitalization of "Woman" and "Man" in English versions, Adam employed a new word for "man" that has not occurred throughout the creation story thus far. Although it is his proper name, the Hebrew word "Adam" also simply means "man." This word also sounds very similar to the Hebrew word for "ground," namely "*adamah*."

Remember, Adam was a gardener, so his job was to work the ground, albeit without toil before the fall. Previously, the narrative named Adam in relation to the ground, recounting how Adam (אָדָם, *adam*) comes from the *adamah* (אֲדָמָה), closely associating him with his work. Now, however, Adam changes terminology, naming himself, the man, in relation to his wife, the woman: the *'ish* (אִישׁ) in relation to the *'ishah* (אִשָּׁה).[9] Adam then reprioritized his self-description to highlight how his fundamental relationship was with his wife rather than his work.

These textual points, although fine details, nonetheless carry significant practical weight. For husbands especially, how many times do we invert that order and define ourselves by our work rather than by our relationship with our wife? Do you think of yourself foremost by connection to the task God has given you or by the communion God has granted you in marriage? Each of us, husband or wife, easily lets our relationships begin to focus on the jobs we have, the house where we live, the activities in which we engage, the way that we do this and that. In other words, many distractions potentially threaten to invade our marriages and begin to dissolve that relationship as our fundamental calling. We need to exhort ourselves to remember that our marriages are about communion. Just because work is draining does not mean that time at home is for tuning out and vegging on television or that you have done your part and can tick the box. Marriage is about communion. We should live like it. Practicing communion means involving our full selves continually in the relationship of marriage.

PRIORITIZING COMMUNION

As we have seen, God's purpose for marriage to portray rich communion has an ethical bearing on our lives, whether we are married or not. Now we need to reflect on how marriage calls us to consider how we prioritize our relationships. Moses, as Genesis' author, almost entirely omitted any comment of his own from this account of the world's origins. Throughout this narrative, any injunctions or commands are spoken by God, putting any normative instructions on the Lord's lips. But there is one exception.

The narrative itself angles toward its conclusion concerning Adam's marriage to Eve with an inference from Adam's declaration of joy over his newfound wife. Following on Adam's statement of his close connection to his wife, *Moses* enjoins, as his single narrator's intrusion in this account, a programmatic statement about marriage based on the fittingness of the woman for the man: "Therefore a man shall leave his father and his mother and hold fast to his wife, and they shall become one flesh" (Genesis 2:24). That Moses would interrupt his story to drop this inference highlights its unique and emphatic value as a crucial ethical summons for God's people as we read this text.

This ethical payoff of the marriage account highlights how we must actively work to prioritize the right relationships. This intimate bond of leaving and holding fast to one another explains why Adam and Eve were naked and unashamed together. More fundamentally, this marriage bond takes precedence over biological family relationships.[10] Although certainly we maintain our loving commitment to our parents and relatives, our marriage relocates us from a primary connection to those relationships to a priority on our marriage. Godly parents will remain continual fonts of wisdom for us, but you cannot allow your biological links to create any division in your marriage or have any dominance over it.

The same goes for children as well. You love your children, undoubtedly, but your marriage is the bedrock of the family. A married couple is a family apart from children, so children need to see the strength of that foundation as the priority in any family.

Just like our identity is shaped by marital communion over our work, so too it is to be shaped by marriage over and before our role as parents.

To be direct, the relevance of this application concerns how often we reorient our relational priorities. Too often, husbands and wives let preexisting family relationships maintain some sort of trump card over the marital bond. Whether a husband lets his mother have too much space and sway between him and his wife or a wife continually measures her husband against her father (or some other disproportioned situation exemplified in these common situations), both parties face potential dangers of letting some other family relationship interfere with the priority of the marriage. If the Lord in his providence blesses a couple with kids, recognizing that infertility and other issues cause pain for an increasing number of couples, both husbands and wives can wrestle not to let their kids become the priority over the marriage. Certainly, we cannot neglect our children, nor is this point meant to disparage the love we should give to our kids. Nonetheless, we must still prioritize our marriages, especially never letting our children set us against each other in any way. This application certainly plays into what it means to manage a household well with submissive children (1 Timothy 3:4).

Marriage teaches us to prioritize our relationships, extending to how we must learn to prioritize our communion with God in Christ. After all, Scripture very plainly states that marriage depicts Christ's relationship to his church, further providing a theological ground for prioritizing our marriages (Ephesians 5:22–33). Just like marriage relocates you from the primary link to your biological family into that covenantal bond, so too faith in Christ relocates you from a natural link to the world into that covenantal bond with the Savior. Just like personal communion in marriage takes priority to enable raising children well, so too our personal communion with Christ takes priority to enable us to disciple others well in our families or among friends.

Marriage leads us to contemplate the riches of the gospel itself. Pointedly, it takes two people who were once separate and joins them together in communion by covenant. In contrast with marriage joining two people who formerly had no bond of this sort, sinners are alienated and estranged from God as his enemies. Still, the gospel provides the means of being restored to communion with God.

In this respect, Christ the Savior is our most rich and faithful husband. His immense love as our bridegroom is clear in how vigorously he pursued us. In our state of sin, we preferred the refuse of the world, favoring one-night stands with our wretched desires more than we desired the unbridled and faithful love of God. Thankfully, Christ, the faithful husband to his church, came and died for every sin of every believer, so that he might cleanse us and make us blameless to present us spotless on the last day at his return, when we will have the wedding feast of the lamb and celebrate the consummate communion of Christ and his people.

CONCLUSION

It is not good for man to be alone, so marriage is good, but marriage to Christ is best, regardless of your marital status.[11] In Christ, we are never alone and have the very communion for which we were created: union with our God. As Adam leaped for joy to claim Eve as his bride, Christ for the joy set before him endured the cross to claim us as his bride (Hebrews 12:2). The depth of communion we see in faithful marriages was forged into creation in order to point us to the communion that we have with God in Christ. Every joy that is displayed for us all in marriage, as hard as it is to fathom, is dwarfed by the overwhelming love and communion that we have with our Maker because of Christ.

QUESTIONS FOR FURTHER REFLECTION

1. Males and females are created distinctly different but uniquely in a fashion to share intimate communion. How does this reflect our relationship with our Creator?

2. When you meet a stranger, do you introduce and identify yourself by your vocation? How should our most intimate relationships inform our identity?

3. How does understanding the unique communion we have with our spouse prioritize other relationships?

4. How does marriage cause us to contemplate the riches of the Gospel?

A CALL TO COMMUNION

The Creator at the Heart of Creation

When he pastored at St. Pierre's Cathedral, John Calvin began services every Sunday with the call to worship: "Our help is in the name of the Lord, who made heaven and earth" (Psalm 124:8). Why would the Genevan reformer believe that God's people would benefit from this pronouncement so often? Our reflections on Genesis' opening chapters should help us see why we would take great heart in having the God who fashioned the universe as our shelter.

Although we may often come to Genesis 1–2 with other questions, this little book has tried to prove that these chapters' main point is the glorious God and our relationship with him. God fashioned the earth, authoring order and bringing beauty within the world, to prepare an environment and a kingdom for his people to live in and rule. God created humanity in his image, fit for communion with him, to reflect his character into his creation. God then appointed a time and a place for his image bearers to commune with him. He entered into covenant with us, giving marriage to us as a covenant as well, so that we would learn about the depth of what communion can be. God, therefore, worked over his creation to orient all things toward communion with his people. To find our help in the Lord who made heaven and earth is to have protection and provision from the God whose external acts all stream together in glorifying himself by forging an everlasting relationship with us.

The creation narrative of Genesis 1–2, however much it might say about creation, is primarily about the Creator. Our hearts should be enflamed with love and worship as we read the unfolding drama of God crafting the universe so that we might know his love and glorify him for it. In this way, Genesis 1–2 addresses God's covenant people as a call to communion with our God. The amazing days of creation's first moment recount how God summoned things that had no being into existence so that creatures might enjoy their Maker. Inasmuch as the creation account addresses God's people to confront us with God's glory, it tells us of his love for us, and direct us to Christ in the gospel. The call to communion in Genesis 1–2 reminds God's people today that all those in Christ still live in and still wait for extraordinary days.

ACKNOWLEDGMENTS

Since writing and proposing this book, I accepted a call at Oakland Hills Community Church (OPC), where I am now happy to be their pastor, moving from my previous pastoral post at London City Presbyterian Church. Nonetheless, this book is dedicated to the elders (teaching and ruling) from both sessions because they have all contributed to making the pastoral task a delight. I do not take it for granted that I have had back-to-back experiences of serving with extraordinary elders. I know that this blessing is rare and thank God constantly for putting me in the company of these men who sacrificially labor Christ and his people, who have loved and shepherded me and my family, and who are stalwart examples of godliness and service. I hope God might use me to bless others even half as much as you have blessed me. John Frith, Mark Hakim, Mark Rebhan, Greg Weigler, Dick Haffenden, Andy Longwe, Adam de Jong, Gabriel Amorim, and Bob Akroyd, in my eyes, you all are superheroes, titans of the faith, and it is my ever-humbling honor to have served with you men.

During the COVID-19 pandemic of 2020, which took a heavy toll on the world but created perhaps unique difficulties for congregation that prioritizes being together yet spread across greater London in strict lockdown, the obvious need was a focus on God's majesty. Whereas that moment could easily provoke concentration on our own setting, speculation about the future, or practical concerns for "lockdown living," it seemed more important to me to have our focus lifted above the present troubles to God's greatness that transcends all our circumstances. So, I began to preach on communion with God. The research that most grabbed my attention was how Genesis 1–2 so plainly and thoroughly teaches about our fellowship with the Lord even from creation. Hence, this book is the fruit of continual reflection upon those themes and how they might help the people of God.

Thanks need to go those members of LCPC who encouraged me to continue to work on this research to ready it for a wider audience, especially Jan Campbell and Eduard Roos for originating the idea. Thanks also to J.V. Fesko; Greg Weigler; my mom, Denise Perkins; LCPC's wonderful church administrator, Laura Bol; Bob Akroyd; Tony Faggiano; and Chad Vegas for reading over the first draft. Thanks also to Todd Hains and the Lexham team who do an excellent job at producing books and make the process easy on authors. Of course, I need to thank my wife, Sarah, for her continual support every time I set myself to some new writing project. Her love is of endless encouragement and joy to me. Finally, I pray that the Lord will bless this book to encourage God's people who also may need something to lift their heads above our bleak horizon to the grandeur of our majestic God and his work for us in Christ.

NOTES

CHAPTER 1: AN INVITATION TO COMMUNION

1. Francis Petrarch, "On the Nature of Poetry: To His Brother Gherardo," in James Harvey Robinson, *Petrarch: The First Modern Scholar and Man of Letters* (New York and London: The Knickerbocker Press, 1909), 261.
2. Giovanni Boccaccio, *Tratatello in Laude di Dante,* trans. Vincenzo Zin Bollettino (New York: Garland Publishing, 1990), 41 (emphasis added).

CHAPTER 2: CRAFTED FOR COMMUNION

1. Hans Boersma, *Scripture as Real Presence: Sacramental Exegesis in the Early Church* (Grand Rapids: Baker Academic, 2017).
2. R. C. Sproul, ed., *Reformation Study Bible* (Orlando, FL: Reformation Trust, 2015), 2465. I have modernized the verb tenses in this quote. All confessional citations come from the *Reformation Study Bible.*
3. David C. Hagopian (ed.), *The Genesis Debate: Three Views of Creation* (Mission Viejo, CA: Crux Press, 2000); Joseph A. Pipa Jr. and David W. Hall (eds.), *Did God Create in 6 Days?* (White Hall, WV: Tolle Lege Press, 1999); Ronald L. Numbers, *The Creationists: From Scientific Creationism to Intelligent Design,* expanded ed. (Cambridge, MA: Harvard University Press, 2006).
4. John Calvin, *Commentaries on the First Book of Moses Called Genesis,* trans. John King, 2 vol. (Edinburgh: Calvin Translation Society, 1847), 1:79.
5. Herman Bavinck, *The Wonderful Works of God,* trans. Henry Zylstra (Glenside, PA: Westminster Seminary Press, 2019), 2.
6. Geerhardus Vos, *Reformed Dogmatics,* trans. and ed. Richard B. Gaffin Jr., 5 vol. (Bellingham, WA: Lexham Press, 2012–14), 1:161.
7. John D. Currid, *Against the Gods: The Polemical Theology of the Old Testament* (Wheaton, IL: Crossway, 2013), 11–46.

8. Without adopting all his conclusions or applications, I have taken this layer cake illustration from John Walton, *The Lost World of Genesis One: Ancient Cosmology and the Origins Debate* (Downers Grove, IL: IVP Academic, 2009), 113–17.

CHAPTER 3: THE BEGINNING OF COMMUNION

1. My translation, drawing attention to the waw disjunctive at the beginning of verse 2; Gordon J. Wenham, *Genesis 1–15*, Word Biblical Commentary (Grand Rapids: Zondervan, 1987), 15; Henri Blocher, *In the Beginning: The Opening Chapters of Genesis* (Downers Grove, IL: IVP Academic, 1984), 43.
2. Bruce K. Waltke with Cathi J. Fredericks, *Genesis: A Commentary* (Grand Rapids: Zondervan, 2001), 58; John H. Walton, *The Lost World of Genesis One: Ancient Cosmology and the Origins Debate* (Downers Grove, IL: IVP Academic, 2009), 36–45; possibly John D. Currid, *Genesis*, 2 vol., EP Study Commentary (Holywell, UK: Evangelical Press, 2003), 1:56, although he rejected many aspects that tend to accompany this interpretation.
3. As summarized in Currid, *Genesis*, 1:56.
4. Walton, *Lost World of Genesis One*, 46–52.
5. Walton, *Lost World of Genesis One*, 92–98.
6. Douglas F. Kelly, *Creation and Change: Genesis 1.1–2.4 in the Light of Changing Scientific Paradigms*, revised and updated edition (Fearn, UK: Mentor, 2017), 73–96; C. John Collins, *Genesis 1–4: A Linguistic, Literary, and Theological Commentary* (Philipsburg, NJ: P&R, 2006), 78; Wenham, *Genesis 1–15*, 17; Lane G. Tipton, *Foundations of Covenant Theology: A Biblical-Theological Study of Genesis 1–3* (Philadelphia: Reformed Forum, 2021), 33–41.
7. Vern S. Poythress, *Interpreting Eden: A Guide to Faithfully Reading and Understanding Genesis 1–3* (Wheaton, IL: Crossway, 2019), 291–322; Derek Kidner, *Genesis*, Tyndale Old Testament Commentaries (Downers Grove, IL: IVP Academic, 1967; repr. 2008), 48; Collins, *Genesis 1–4*, 50–55.
8. Joel R. Beeke and Paul M. Smalley, *Reformed Systematic Theology Volume 2: Man and Christ* (Wheaton, IL: Crossway, 2020), 62.

9. John Calvin, *Commentaries on the First Book of Moses Called Genesis*, trans. John King, 2 vol. (Edinburgh: Calvin Translation Society, 1847), 1:70.

10. Petrus van Mastricht, *Theoretical-Practical Theology: Volume 3: The Works of God and the Fall of Man*, trans. Todd M. Rester, ed. Joel R. Beeke (Grand Rapids: Reformation Heritage Books, 2021), 179–80, 189; Tipton, *Foundations of Covenant Theology*; 33–41; Beeke and Smalley, *Reformed Systematic Theology* 2, 62; Kelly, *Creation and Change*, 118.

11. Beeke and Smalley, *Reformed Systematic Theology* 2, 67–68.

12. van Mastricht, *Theoretical-Practical Theology* 3, 125, 143–56.

13. Kidner, *Genesis*, 47.

14. Calvin, *Genesis*, 1:76.

15. Beeke and Smalley, *Reformed Systematic Theology* 2, 68.

16. Matthew Barrett, *None Greater: The Undomesticated Attributes of God* (Grand Rapids: Baker, 2019), 55–69.

17. St. Thomas Aquinas, *Summa Theologica*, trans. Fathers of the English Dominican Province, 5 vol. (Notre Dame, IN: Christian Classics, 1948), 1.46.2.

18. Aristotle, *The Physics*, trans. Philip H. Wicksteed and Francis M. Cornford, 2 vol. (London and New York: William Heinemann LTD and G. P. Putnam's Sons, 1929), §2.1 (pg. 1:113).

19. James E. Dolezal, *All that is in God: Evangelical Theology and the Challenge of Classical Christian Theism* (Grand Rapids: Reformation Heritage Books, 2017), 79–104.

20. Thanks to Bob Akroyd for this application.

21. Beeke and Smalley, *Reformed Systematic Theology* 2, 61.

22. Geerhardus Vos, "Jeremiah's Plaint and Its Answer," in *Redemptive History and Biblical Interpretation: The Shorter Writings of Geerhardus Vos*, ed. Richard B. Gaffin Jr. (Phillipsburg, NJ: P&R Publishing, 2001), 298.

CHAPTER 4: EFFECTIVE COMMUNION

1. Douglas F. Kelly, *Creation and Change: Genesis 1.1–2.4 in the Light of Changing Scientific Paradigms*, rev. and updated ed. (Fearn, UK: Mentor, 2017), 236, 267–68.

2. Derek Kidner, *Genesis*, Tyndale Old Testament Commentary (Downers Grove, IL: IVP Academic, 1967, repr. 2008), 50.
3. C. John Collins, *Genesis 1–4: A Linguistic, Literary, and Theological Commentary* (Philipsburg, NJ: P&R, 2006), 78; Gordon J. Wenham, *Genesis 1–15*, Word Biblical Commentary (Grand Rapids: Zondervan, 1987), 17.
4. John H. Walton, *The Lost World of Genesis One: Ancient Cosmology and the Origins Debate* (Downers Grove, IL: IVP Academic, 2009), 46–70; John H. Walton, *The Lost World of Adam and Eve: Genesis 2–3 and the Human Origins Debate* (Downers Grove, IL: IVP Academic, 2015), 24–45. Even as I appropriate Walton's point that God gave function to various features of the universe during the creation week, I reject that this point means that God was not also performing acts of material creation, *especially* in reference to Genesis 1:1. Although Walton has perhaps not absolutely suggested a false dichotomy between material creation and functional assignments, I do believe that he has argued for one side of the coin at the expense of the other when both should be held together *at least* in some measure.
5. Vern S. Poythress, *Interpreting Eden: A Guide to Faithfully Reading and Understanding Genesis 1–3* (Wheaton, IL: Crossway, 2019), 213–46.
6. Kelly, *Creation and Change*, 152, 154.
7. John Calvin, *Commentaries on the First Book of Moses Called Genesis*, trans. John King, 2 vol. (Edinburgh: Calvin Translation Society, 1847), 1:78.
8. Thanks to Tim Sullivan, member at Oakland Hills Community Church (OPC), for making this point.
9. Calvin, *Genesis*, 1:80–81; Wenham, *Genesis 1–15*, 19; Collins, *Genesis 1–4*, 45–46n23, 46n24; Poythress, *Interpreting Eden*, 171–86, 341–54; Petrus van Mastricht, *Theoretical-Practical Theology: Volume 3: The Works of God and the Fall of Man*, trans. Todd M. Rester, ed. Joel R. Beeke (Grand Rapids: Reformation Heritage Books, 2021), 165, 170; Bruce K. Waltke with Cathi J. Fredericks, *Genesis: A Commentary* (Grand Rapids: Zondervan, 2001), 62.
10. Henri Blocher, *In the Beginning: The Opening Chapters of Genesis* (Downers Grove, IL: IVP Academic, 1984), 49.
11. Collins, *Genesis 1–4*, 77.

12. G. K. Beale, *The Temple and the Church's Mission: A Biblical Theology of the Dwelling Place of God,* New Studies in Biblical Theology (Downers Grove, IL: IVP Academic, 2004), 29–122.
13. R. C. Sproul, ed., *Reformation Study Bible* (Orlando, FL: Reformation Trust, 2015), 2473 (emphasis added).

CHAPTER 5: BEAUTIFUL COMMUNION

1. Derek Kidner, *Genesis,* Tyndale Old Testament Commentary (Downers Grove, IL: IVP Academic, 1967, repr. 2008), 50.
2. E. J. Young, *The Book of Isaiah,* 3 vol. (Grand Rapids: Eerdmans, 1972), 3:211; Douglas F. Kelly, *Creation and Change: Genesis 1.1–2.4 in the Light of Changing Scientific Paradigms,* rev. and updated ed. (Fearn, UK: Mentor, 2017), 121.
3. The narrative of verse 3 picks up *sometime* after verses 1–2; Gordon J. Wenham, *Genesis 1–15,* Word Biblical Commentary (Grand Rapids: Zondervan, 1987), 17; C. John Collins, *Genesis 1–4: A Linguistic, Literary, and Theological Commentary* (Philipsburg, NJ: P&R, 2006), 78.
4. Bruce K. Waltke with Cathi J. Fredericks, *Genesis: A Commentary* (Grand Rapids: Zondervan, 2001), 60; Wenham, *Genesis 1–15,* 16.
5. John Calvin, *Commentaries on the First Book of Moses Called Genesis,* trans. John King, 2 vol. (Edinburgh: Calvin Translation Society, 1847), 1:80–81; Vern S. Poythress, *Interpreting Eden: A Guide to Faithfully Reading and Understanding Genesis 1–3* (Wheaton, IL: Crossway, 2019), 171–86, 341–54; Collins, *Genesis 1–4,* 45–46n23, 46n24; Wenham, *Genesis 1–15,* 19; Waltke with Fredericks, *Genesis,* 62.
6. Kelly, *Creation and Change,* 261–62.
7. St. Augustine, *The Literal Meaning of Genesis,* trans. John Hammond Taylor, 2 vol. (New York: Newman Press, 1982), 4.33.51–52 (italics original). Calvin likely had Augustine in mind when he argued, as quoted in the previous chapter, against instantaneous creation; Calvin, *Genesis,* 1:78.
8. D. Glen Butner Jr., *Trinitarian Dogmatics: Exploring the Grammar of the Christian Doctrine of God* (Grand Rapids: Baker Academic, 2022), 133–51.
9. Calvin, *Genesis,* 1:98–99.

10. John H. Walton, *The Lost World of Adam and Eve: Genesis 2–3 and the Human Origins Debate* (Downers Grove, IL: IVP Academic, 2015), 82–89; Wenham, *Genesis 1–15*, 9.
11. John Calvin, *Sermons on Genesis: Chapters 1–11*, trans. Roy McGregor (Edinburgh: The Banner of Truth Trust, 2009), 90. Thanks to Chad Vegas for this quote.
12. Meredith G. Kline, *Kingdom Prologue: Genesis Foundations for a Covenantal Worldview* (Overland Park, KS: Two Age Press, 2000), 54–55; Waltke with Fredericks, *Genesis*, 84.
13. Calvin, *Genesis*, 1:98–100; 291–93; Gavin Ortlund, *Retrieving Augustine's Doctrine of Creation: Ancient Wisdom for Current Controversy* (Downers Grove, IL: IVP Academic, 2020), 151–82; St. Thomas Aquinas, *Summa Theologica*, trans. by Fathers of the English Dominican Province, 5 vol. (New York, NY: Benziger Bros., 1948; repr. Notre Dame, IN: Christian Classics, 1981), 1.96.1 ad 2; Collins, *Genesis 1–4*, 165; Wenham, *Genesis 1–15*, 34; Kidner, *Genesis*, 57; Herman Bavinck, *Reformed Dogmatics*, trans. John Vriend, ed. John Bolt, 4 vol. (Grand Rapids: Baker Academic, 2003–8), 2:575.
14. Henri Blocher, *In the Beginning: The Opening Chapters of Genesis* (Downers Grove, IL: IVP Academic, 1984), 42.
15. David VanDrunen, *Bioethics and the Christian Life: A Guide to Making Difficult Decisions* (Wheaton, IL: Crossway, 2009), 147–68.
16. Wenham, *Genesis 1–15*, 176–77.
17. Calvin, *Genesis*, 1:291–92.
18. כָּל־רֶמֶשׂ
19. בְּכָל־הַשֶּׁרֶץ הָרֹמֵשׂ
20. Thanks to Byron Weigler for raising questions about this point to help me think through the issue in Genesis 9:3.

CHAPTER 6: MADE FOR COMMUNION

1. The specific idea of a *relational* point of contact protects the Creator-creature distinction by not suggesting any true overlap of God and creation in some point of contact between God's essence and ours. The contact is in God specially designing us for relational communion with him.

2. Douglas F. Kelly, *Creation and Change: Genesis 1.1–2.4 in the Light of Changing Scientific Paradigms*, rev. and updated ed. (Fearn, UK: Mentor, 2017), 285–88.
3. R. C. Sproul, ed., *Reformation Study Bible* (Orlando, FL: Reformation Trust, 2015), 2471.
4. Michael Horton, *The Christian Faith: A Systematic Theology for Pilgrims on the Way* (Grand Rapids: Zondervan, 2011), 389.
5. Horton, *Christian Faith*, 389.
6. Geerhardus Vos, *Grace and Glory: Sermons Preached at Princeton Seminary* (East Peoria, IL: The Banner of Truth Trust, 2020), 36.
7. I have elaborated on this material about virtue in Harrison Perkins, "Virtue Is Its Own Reward," *Modern Reformation*, September 8, 2020, https://www.modernreformation.org/resources/articles/the-mod-virtue-is-its-own-reward.

CHAPTER 7: A TIME FOR COMMUNION

1. Thanks to Bob Akroyd for his insight on this point.
2. R. C. Sproul, ed., *Reformation Study Bible* (Orlando, FL: Reformation Trust, 2015), 2471.
3. *Reformation Study Bible*, 2476.
4. C. John Collins, *Genesis 1–4: A Linguistic, Literary, and Theological Commentary* (Phillipsburg, NJ: P&R, 2006), 89–90.

CHAPTER 8: A PLACE FOR COMMUNION

1. John D. Currid, *Genesis*, 2 vol., EP Study Commentary (Holywell, UK: Evangelical Press, 2003), 94–95; Derek Kidner, *Genesis*, Tyndale Old Testament Commentaries (Downers Grove, IL: IVP Academic, 1967), 25–26, 64; Bruce K. Waltke with Cathi J. Fredericks, *Genesis: A Commentary* (Grand Rapids: Zondervan, 2001), 83; Gordon J. Wenham, *Genesis 1–15*, Word Biblical Commentary (Grand Rapids: Zondervan, 1987), 49–50, 55–57.
2. C. John Collins, "Discourse Analysis and the Interpretation of Gen 2:4–7," *Westminster Theological Journal* 61 (1999): 269–76.
3. Currid, *Genesis*, 1:96; C. John Collins, *Genesis 1–4: A Linguistic, Literary, and Theological Commentary* (Philipsburg, NJ: P&R, 2006), 109–11, 126;

Meredith G. Kline, "Because It Had Not Rained," *Westminster Theological Journal* 20 no 2 (May 1958): 149–50; Mark D. Futato, "Because It Had Rained: A Study of Gen 2:5–7 with Implications for Gen 2:4–25 and Gen 1:1–2:3," *Westminster Theological Journal* 60 no 1 (1998): 1, 3–5, 6.

4. John Calvin, *Commentaries on the First Book of Moses Called Genesis*, trans. John King, 2 vol. (Edinburgh: Calvin Translation Society, 1847), 1:80–81; Vern S. Poythress, *Interpreting Eden: A Guide to Faithfully Reading and Understanding Genesis 1–3* (Wheaton, IL: Crossway, 2019), 171–86, 341–54; Henri Blocher, *In the Beginning: The Opening Chapters of Genesis* (Downers Grove, IL: IVP Academic, 1987), 53–56; Collins, *Genesis 1–4*, 45–46n23, 46n24; Wenham, *Genesis 1–15*, 19; Waltke with Fredericks, *Genesis*, 62.

5. John H. Walton, *The Lost World of Adam and Eve: Genesis 2–3 and the Human Origins Debate* (Downers Grove, IL: IVP Academic, 2015), 18.

6. Collins, *Genesis 1–4*, 111, 125–28; Futato, "Because It Had Rained," 3–5, esp. 3n8.

7. Kline, "Because It Had Not Rained," 150n7; Futato, "Because It Had Rained," 5; Collins, "Discourse Analysis," 274–75.

8. Futato, "Because It Had Rained," 5.

9. Collins, *Genesis 1–4*, 104n6, 108–12, 126–27; Futato, "Because It Had Rained" 5– 10; Franz Delitzch, *A New Commentary on Genesis*, trans. Sophia Taylor, 2 vol. (Edinburgh: T&T Clark, 1888), 117; Mitchell Dahood, "Eblaite í-du and Hebrew ʾēd, 'Rain-Cloud,'" *The Catholic Biblical Quarterly* 43 no 4 (1981) 534–38; cf. Derek Kidner, "Genesis 2:5, 6: Wet or Dry?" *Tyndale Bulletin* 17 (1966): 109–14.

10. Futato, "Because It Had Rained," 5.

11. G. K. Beale, *The Temple and the Church's Mission: A Biblical Theology of the Dwelling Place of God*, New Studies in Biblical Theology (Downers Grove, IL: IVP Academic, 2004), 81–122.

12. G. K. Beale, *The Book of Revelation*, New International Greek Testament Commentary (Grand Rapids: Eerdmans, 1999), 1103–11; Richard C. Barcellos, *Getting the Garden Right: Adam's Work and God's Rest in Light of Christ* (Cape Coral, FL: Founders Press, 2017), 150–51.

13. Walton, *Lost World of Adam and Eve*, 117.

14. Walton, *Lost World of Adam and Eve*, 215n4.

15. Beale, *Revelation*, 1087–88, 1090.

16. G. K. Beale and Mitchell Kim, *God Dwells Among Us: Expanding Eden to the Ends of the Earth* (Downers Grove, IL: IVP Academic, 2015), 23. Thanks to Scott McDermand for directing me to this point.
17. Beale, *The Book of Revelation*, 1110–11; Wenham, *Genesis 1–15*, 67; J. V. Fesko, *Last Things First: Unlocking Genesis 1–3 with the Christ of Eschatology* (Fearn: Mentor, 2007), 71–73; Benjamin L. Gladd, *From Adam and Israel to the Church: A Biblical Theology of the People of God* (Essential Studies in Biblical Theology; Downers Grove, IL: IVP Academic, 2019), 15–18; Walton, *Lost World of Adam and Eve*, 104–15; Lane G. Tipton, *Foundations of Covenant Theology: A Biblical-Theological Study of Genesis 1–3* (Philadelphia: Reformed Forum, 2021), 90–91.
18. Thanks to my friend Tim Graham, who pointed out this connection regarding cherubim.
19. Meredith G. Kline, *Kingdom Prologue: Genesis Foundations for a Covenantal Worldview* (Overland Park, KS: Two Ages Press, 2000), 121, 128.
20. Thanks to J. V. Fesko for this point.
21. Geerhardus Vos, *Grace and Glory: Sermons Preached at Princeton Seminary* (East Peoria, IL: The Banner of Truth Trust, 2020), 21–22.
22. Kim Riddlebarger, "The Reformation of the Supper," in *Always Reformed: Essays in Honor of W. Robert Godfrey*, ed. R. Scott Clark and Joel E. Kim (Escondido, CA: Westminster Seminary California, 2010), 192–98.
23. Zach Keele, "The Slaying of the Dragon," *Modern Reformation*, April 11, 2022, https://www.modernreformation.org/resources/articles/the-mod-the-slaying-of-the-dragon-revelation-127-12.
24. Beale, *Revelation*, 1111.

CHAPTER 9: COMMUNION BY COVENANT

1. Meredith G. Kline, *Kingdom Prologue: Genesis Foundations for a Covenantal Worldview* (Overland Park, KS: Two Age Press, 2000), 54–55; Bruce K. Waltke with Cathi J. Fredericks, *Genesis: A Commentary* (Grand Rapids, MI: Zondervan, 2001), 84.
2. Gordon J. Wenham, *Genesis 1–15*, Word Biblical Commentary (Grand Rapids: Zondervan, 1987), 56–57; Waltke with Fredericks, *Genesis*, 84; Peter J. Gentry and Stephen J. Wellum, *Kingdom Through Covenant: A*

Biblical-Theological Understanding of the Covenants, 2nd ed. (Wheaton, IL: Crossway, 2018), 215–16.

3. Geerhardus Vos, *Reformed Dogmatics*, trans. and ed. Richard B. Gaffin Jr., 5 vol. (Bellingham, WA: Lexham Press, 2012–14), 2:46.

4. Vos, *Reformed Dogmatics*, 2:48.

5. John Calvin, *Commentaries on the First Book of Moses Called Genesis*, trans. John King, 2 vol. (Edinburgh: Calvin Translation Society, 1847), 1:125–26. I have improved the translation of this edition in consultation with the original Latin: John Calvin, *Opera quae superunt omnia*, ed. Edouard Cunitz, Johann-Wilhem Baum, and Eduard Wilhem Eugen Reuss, 58 vol., Corpus Reformatorum (Brunsigae: C.A. Schwetschke, 1863), 23:44 (*Docet nunc Moses, cum hac exceptione hominem fuisse terrae praefectum, ut tamen Deo subesset. Lex illi in signum subiectionis imponitur: nam Dei nihil intererat, illum promiscue quolibet fructu vesci. Ergo unius arboris prohibitio obsequie examen fuit … Ideo abstinentia ab unius arboris fructu obedientiae quoddam fuit rudimentum: ut sciret homo habere se rectorem vitae ac dominum, a cuius nutu pendere, et cuius acquiescere iussis deberet*).

6. Henri Blocher, *In the Beginning: The Opening Chapters of Genesis* (Downers Grove, IL: IVP Academic, 1984), 126–33.

7. C. John Collins, *Genesis 1–4: A Linguistic, Literary, and Theological Commentary* (Philipsburg, NJ: P&R, 2006), 112–14; Blocher, *In the Beginning*, 133–34.

8. John D. Currid, *Genesis*, 2 vol., EP Study Commentary (Holywell, UK: Evangelical Press, 2003), 1:105–6; Derek Kidner, *Genesis*, Tyndale Old Testament Commentaries (Downers Grove, IL: IVP Academic, 1967; repr. 2008), 67–70; Waltke with Fredericks, *Genesis*, 84–88; Vos, *Reformed Dogmatics*, 2:41–49.

9. Vos, *Reformed Dogmatics*, 2:225–28; Herman Bavinck, *Reformed Dogmatics*, ed. John Bolt, trans. John Vriend, 4 vol. (Grand Rapids: Baker Academic, 2003–8), 2:564; Peter Jones, "Paul Confronts Paganism in the Church. A Case Study of First Corinthians 15:45," *Journal of the Evangelical Theological Society* 49, no. 4 (December 2006): 713–27; Richard B. Gaffin Jr., *Resurrection and Redemption: A Study on Paul's Soteriology* (Phillipsburg, NJ: P&R, 1987), 80, 85–89, 108–12; Charles Hodge, *1 & 2 Corinthians*, Geneva Series Commentaries (Bath, UK: Banner of Truth, 1974; repr. 2000), 349–51; Gordon D. Fee, *The First*

Epistle to the Corinthians, rev. ed., New International Commentary on the New Testament (Grand Rapids: Eerdmans, 2014), 872–75; Anthony C. Thistleton, *The First Epistle to the Corinthians*, New International Greek Testament Commentary (Grand Rapids: Eerdmans, 2000), 1281–85.
10. G. K. Beale, "Adam as the First Priest in Eden as the Garden Temple," *Southern Baptist Journal of Theology* 22, no 2 (2018): 11–13
11. G. K. Beale and Mitchell Kim, *God Dwells Among Us: Expanding Eden to the Ends of the Earth* (Downers Grove, IL: Intervarsity Press, 2014), 21.
12. Beale and Kim, *God Dwells Among Us*, 17–28.
13. Beale, "Adam as the First Priest," 20.

CHAPTER 10: CREATURELY COMMUNION

1. Saint Hilary of Poitiers, *The Trinity*, trans. Stephen McKenna (Washington, DC: The Catholic University of America Press, 1954), 176.
2. Gregory Nazianzen, *The Fifth Theological Oration: On the Holy Spirit*, §31; in *Nicene and Post-Nicene Fathers, Second Series Volume VII*, ed. Philip Schaff and Henry Wace (New York: Christian Literature Company, 1894), 328.
3. Augustine, *On the Holy Trinity*, 6.10.12; in *Nicene and Post-Nicene Fathers Volume III*, ed. Philip Schaff (Buffalo, NY: Christian Literature Company, 1887), 103.
4. Joel R. Beeke and Paul M. Smalley, *Reformed Systematic Theology Volume 1: Revelation and God* (Wheaton, IL: Crossway, 2019), 195–212.
5. Robert Letham, *Systematic Theology* (Wheaton, IL: Crossway, 2019), 128–30.
6. Augustine, *On the Holy Trinity*, 7.6.12, in Schaff, *Nicene and Post-Nicene Fathers III*, 113.
7. John Calvin, *Commentaries on the First Book of Moses Called Genesis*, trans. John King, 2 vol. (Edinburgh: Calvin Translation Society, 1847), 1:93. Calvin criticized primarily Augustine's argument in *On the Holy Trinity*, 10.1–12, in Schaff, *Nicene and Post-Nicene Fathers III*, 134–45.
8. Thomas Aquinas, *Summa Theologica*, trans. Fathers of the English Dominican Province, 5 vol. (Notre Dame, IN: Christian Classics, 1948), 1.12.4, 12.
9. Herman Bavinck, *Reformed Dogmatics*, ed. John Bolt, trans. John Vriend, 4 vol. (Grand Rapids: Baker Academic, 2003–8), 2:333.
10. Thomas, *Summa Theologica*, 1.32.1.

11. Thomas, *Summa Theologica*, 1.45.7
12. Bavinck, *Reformed Dogmatics*, 2:561–62; Andrew Davison, *Participation in God: A Study in Christian Doctrine and Metaphysics* (Cambridge: Cambridge University Press, 2019), 52–58.
13. Bavinck, *Reformed Dogmatics*, 2:303.
14. John D. Currid, *Genesis*, 2 vol., EP Study Commentary (Holywell, UK: Evangelical Press, 2015), 1:93–94; C. John Collins, *Genesis 1–4: A Linguistic, Literary, and Theological Commentary* (Phillipsburg, NJ: P&R, 2006), 109–10, 121–22; cf. John H. Walton, *The Lost World of Adam and Eve: Genesis 2–3 and the Human Origins Debate* (Downers Grove, IL: IVP Academic, 2015), 63–69.
15. Letham, *Systematic Theology*, 108–9.
16. Philip Schaff, ed., *The Creeds of Christendom*, 3 vol. (New York: Harper and Brothers, 1919), 2:66.
17. Douglas F. Kelly, *Systematic Theology Volume One: The God Who Is: The Holy Trinity* (Fearn, UK: Mentor, 2008), 14, 456–57; Bavinck, *Reformed Dogmatics*, 2:301–3.
18. Michael Horton, *The Christian Faith: A Systematic Theology for Pilgrims on the Way* (Grand Rapids: Zondervan, 2011), 275–76. Horton underscores the point that the *analogy* between the interpenetrating relationships among the persons of the Godhead (perichoresis) and human relationships does not entail social trinitarianism. The point is, after all, not that we are identical to God in this communal way but merely that there is an analogy; Horton, *Christian Faith*, 296–99.
19. Douglas F. Kelly, *Creation and Change: Genesis 1.1–2.4 in the Light of Changing Scientific Paradigms*, rev. and updated ed. (Fearn, UK: Mentor, 2017), 277–82; J. V. Fesko, *Adam and the Covenant of Works* (Fearn, UK: Mentor, 2021), 419–34; Collins, *Genesis 1–4*, 59–67; Letham, *Systematic Theology*, 70–72; Kelly, *Systematic Theology*, 325, 456–57.
20. Saint Irenaeus, *The Demonstration of the Apostolic Preaching*, trans. J. Armitage Robinson (London and New York: Aeterna Press, 2015), §55.
21. R. C. Sproul, ed., *Reformation Study Bible* (Orlando, FL: Reformation Trust, 2015), 2407–8 (italics original).
22. Kelly, *Creation and Change*, 277.
23. Gordon J. Wenham, *Genesis 1–15*, Word Biblical Commentary (Grand Rapids: Zondervan, 1987), 68.

24. Bruce K. Waltke with Cathi J. Fredericks, *Genesis: A Commentary* (Grand Rapids: Zondervan, 2001), 89; Currid, *Genesis*, 1:108; Collins, *Genesis 1–4*, 138–39.
25. Walton, *Lost World of Adam and Eve*, 104–15.
26. Walton, *Lost World of Adam and Eve*, 111–13.
27. Matthew Barrett, *Simply Trinity: The Unmanipulated Father, Son, and Spirit* (Grand Rapids: Baker Books, 2021), 17–39, 67–93.
28. John D. Currid, "Adam and the Beginning of the Covenant of Grace," in *Covenant Theology: Biblical, Theological, and Historical Perspectives*, ed. Guy Prentiss Waters, J. Nicholas Reid, and John R. Muether (Wheaton, IL: Crossway, 2020), 101.

CHAPTER 11: COMMUNION POINTING TO CHRIST

1. My translation. That God "had already formed" the animals uses the pluperfect tense to note a prior event that had already occurred, but now the narrative resumes with that previous action in view; C. John Collins, *Genesis 1–4: A Linguistic, Literary, and Theological Commentary* (Phillipsburg, NJ: P&R, 2006), 107n27; John D. Currid, *Genesis*, 2 vol., EP Study Commentary (Holywell, UK: Evangelical Press, 2015), 1:108. The waw disjunctive halfway through 2:19, clearly marking the result of Adam's act of naming the animals, further supports the interpretation of the waw disjunction in Genesis 1:2, indicating that the earth's formless and void state was the result of God's *ex nihilo* first creative act.
2. Gordon J. Wenham, *Genesis 1–15*, Word Biblical Commentary (Grand Rapids: Zondervan, 1987), 68; Bruce K. Waltke with Cathi J. Fredericks, *Genesis: A Commentary* (Grand Rapids: Zondervan, 2001), 89; Collins, *Genesis 1–4*, 138–39; Currid, *Genesis*, 1:108–9.
3. Waltke with Fredericks, *Genesis*, 89; Currid, *Genesis*, 1:108; Collins, *Genesis 1–4*, 138–39.
4. Currid, *Genesis*, 1:109.
5. Waltke with Fredericks, *Genesis*, 88.
6. The longest standing view of this passage is that God opened Adam's side and used one of his rib bones to fashion the woman to be his wife; contra John H. Walton, *The Lost World of Adam and Eve: Genesis 2–3 and the Human Origins Debate* (Downers Grove, IL: IVP Academic, 2015), 77–81.
7. Quoted in Wenham, *Genesis 1–15*, 69.

8. Waltke with Fredericks, *Genesis*, 88.
9. Waltke with Fredericks, *Genesis*, 89.
10. Waltke with Fredericks, *Genesis*, 90.
11. Waltke with Fredericks, *Genesis*, 88.

WORKS CITED

Aquinas, St. Thomas. *Summa Theologica.* Translated by Fathers of the English Dominican Province. 5 vol. Notre Dame, IN: Christian Classics, 1948.

Augustine, *The Literal Meaning of Genesis.* Translated by John Hammond Taylor. 2 vol. New York: Newman Press, 1982.

Aristotle. *The Physics,* trans. Philip H. Wicksteed and Francis M. Cornford, 2 vol. London and New York, NY: William Heinemann LTD and G. P. Putnam's Sons, 1929.

Barcellos, Richard C. *Getting the Garden Right: Adam's Work and God's Rest in Light of Christ.* Cape Coral, FL: Founders Press, 2017.

Barrett, Matthew. *None Greater: The Undomesticated Attributes of God.* Grand Rapids: Baker, 2019.

———. *Simply Trinity: The Unmanipulated Father, Son, and Spirit.* Grand Rapids: Baker Books, 2021.

Bavinck, Herman. *Reformed Dogmatics.* Edited by John Bolt, Translated by John Vriend, 4 vol. Grand Rapids: Baker Academic, 2003–8.

———. *The Wonderful Works of God.* Translated by Henry Zylstra. Glenside, PA: Westminster Seminary Press, 2019.

Beale, G. K. "Adam as the First Priest in Eden as the Garden Temple." *Southern Baptist Journal of Theology* 22 no 2 (2018): 9–24.

———. *The Book of Revelation.* New International Greek Testament Commentary. Grand Rapids: Eerdmans, 1999.

———. *The Temple and the Church's Mission: A Biblical Theology of New Studies in Biblical Theology.* Downers Grove, IL: IVP Academic, 2004.

Beale, G. K., and Mitchell Kim. *God Dwells Among Us: Expanding Eden to the Ends of the Earth*. Downers Grove, IL: IVP Academic, 2015.

Beeke, Joel R., and Paul M. Smalley. *Reformed Systematic Theology Volume 1: Revelation and God*. Wheaton, IL: Crossway, 2019.

———. *Reformed Systematic Theology Volume 2: Man and Christ*. Wheaton, IL: Crossway, 2020.

Blocher, Henri. *In the Beginning: The Opening Chapters of Genesis*. Downers Grove, IL: Intervarsity Press, 1984.

Boccaccio. Giovanni. *Tratatello in Laude di Dante*. Translated by Vincenzo Zin Bollettino. New York: Garland Publishing, 1990.

Boersma, Hans. *Scripture as Real Presence: Sacramental Exegesis in the Early Church*. Grand Rapids: Baker Academic, 2017.

Butner Jr., D. Glen. *Trinitarian Dogmatics: Exploring the Grammar of the Christian Doctrine of God*. Grand Rapids: Baker Academic, 2022.

Calvin, John. *Commentaries on the First Book of Moses Called Genesis*. Translated by John King. 2 vol. Edinburgh: Calvin Translation Society, 1847.

———. *Sermons on Genesis: Chapters 1–11*. Translated by Roy McGregor .Edinburgh: The Banner of Truth Trust, 2009.

Clark, R. Scott, and Joel E. Kim, eds. *Always Reformed: Essays in Honor of W. Robert Godfrey*. Escondido, CA: Westminster Seminary California, 2010.

Collins, C. John. "Discourse Analysis and the Interpretation of Gen 2:4–7." *Westminster Theological Journal* 61 (1999): 269–76.

———. *Genesis 1–4: A Linguistic, Literary, and Theological Commentary*. Philipsburg, NJ: P&R, 2006.

Currid, John D. *Against the Gods: The Polemical Theology of the Old Testament*. Wheaton, IL: Crossway, 2013.

———. *Genesis*. 2 vol. EP Study Commentary. Holywell, UK: Evangelical Press, 2003.

Dahood, Mitchell. "Eblaite í-du and Hebrew ʾēd, 'Rain-Cloud.'" *The Catholic Biblical Quarterly* 43 no 4 (Oct 1981): 534–38.

Davison, Andrew. *Participation in God: A Study in Christian Doctrine and Metaphysics*. Cambridge: Cambridge University Press, 2019.

Delitzch, Franz. *A New Commentary on Genesis*. Translated by Sophia Taylor. 2 vol. Edinburgh: T&T Clark, 1888.

Dolezal, James E. *All that is in God: Evangelical Theology and the Challenge of Classical Christian Theism*. Grand Rapids: Reformation Heritage Books, 2017.

Fee, Gordon D. *The First Epistle to the Corinthians*. Rev. ed. New International Commentary on the New Testament. Grand Rapids: Eerdmans, 2014.

Fesko, J. V. *Adam and the Covenant of Works*. Fearn: Mentor, 2021.

———. *Last Things First: Unlocking Genesis with the Christ of Eschatology*. Fearn, UK: Mentor, 2007.

Futato, Mark D. "Because It Had Rained: A Study of Gen 2:5–7 with Implications for Gen 2:4–25 and Gen 1:1–2:3." *Westminster Theological Journal* 60 no 1 (1998): 1–21.

Gaffin Jr., Richard B. *Resurrection and Redemption: A Study on Paul's Soteriology*. Phillipsburg, NJ: P&R, 1987.

Gentry, Peter J., and Stephen J. Wellum. *Kingdom Through Covenant: A Biblical-Theological Understanding of the Covenants*. 2nd ed. Wheaton, IL: Crossway, 2018.

Gladd, Benjamin L. *From Adam and Israel to the Church: A Biblical Theology of the People of God*. Essential Studies in Biblical Theology. Downers Grove, IL: IVP Academic, 2019.

Hilary of Poitiers. *The Trinity*. Translated by Stephen McKenna. Washington, DC: The Catholic University of America Press, 1954.

Hodge, Charles. *1 & 2 Corinthians*. Geneva Series Commentaries. Bath, UK: Banner of Truth, 1974; repr. 2000.

Horton, Michael. *The Christian Faith: A Systematic Theology for Pilgrims on the Way*. Grand Rapids: Zondervan, 2011.

Irenaeus. *The Demonstration of the Apostolic Preaching.* Translated by J. Armitage Robinson. London and New York: Aeterna Press, 2015.

Jones, Peter. "Paul Confronts Paganism in the Church. A Case Study of First Corinthians 15:45," *Journal of the Evangelical Theological Society* 49.4 (December 2006): 713–27.

Kelly, Douglas F. *Creation and Change: Genesis 1.1–2.4 in the Light of Changing Scientific Paradigms.* Revised and updated edition. Fearn, UK: Mentor, 2017.

———. *Systematic Theology Volume One: The God Who Is: The Holy Trinity.* Fearn, UK: Mentor, 2008.

Kidner, Derek. *Genesis.* Tyndale Old Testament Commentaries. Downers Grove, IL: IVP Academic, 1967; repr. 2008.

———. "Genesis 2:5, 6: Wet or Dry?" *Tyndale Bulletin* 17 (1966): 109–14.

Kline, Meredith G. "Because It Had Not Rained," *Westminster Theological Journal* 20 no 2 (May 1958): 146–67.

———. *Kingdom Prologue: Genesis Foundations for a Covenantal Worldview.* Overland Park, KS: Two Age Press, 2000.

Letham, Robert. *Systematic Theology.* Wheaton, IL: Crossway, 2019.

Poythress, Vern S. *Interpreting Eden: A Guide to Faithfully Reading and Understanding Genesis 1–3.* Wheaton, IL: Crossway, 2019.

Robinson, James Harvey. *Petrarch: The First Modern Scholar and Man of Letters.* New York and London: The Knickerbocker Press, 1909.

Schaff, Philip, ed. *The Creeds of Christendom.* 3 vol. New York: Harper and Brothers, 1919.

———. *Nicene and Post-Nicene Fathers Volume III.* Buffalo, NY: Christian Literature Company, 1887.

Schaff, Philip, and Henry Wace, eds. *Nicene and Post-Nicene Fathers, Second Series Volume VII.* New York: Christian Literature Company, 1894.

Thistleton, Anthony C. *The First Epistle to the Corinthians*. New International Greek Testament Commentary. Grand Rapids: Eerdmans, 2000.

Tipton, Lane G. *Foundations of Covenant Theology: A Biblical-Theological Study of Genesis 1–3*. Philadelphia: Reformed Forum, 2021.

VanDrunen, David. *Bioethics and the Christian Life: A Guide to Making Difficult Decisions*. Wheaton, IL: Crossway, 2009.

van Mastricht, Petrus. *Theoretical-Practical Theology: Volume 3: The Works of God and the Fall of Man*. Edited by Joel R. Beeke. Translated by Todd M. Rester. Grand Rapids: Reformation Heritage Books, 2021.

Vos, Geerhardus. *Grace and Glory: Sermons Preached at Princeton Seminary*. East Peoria, IL: The Banner of Truth Trust, 2020.

———. *Redemptive History and Biblical Interpretation: The Shorter Writings of Geerhardus Vos*. ed. Richard B. Gaffin Jr. Phillipsburg, NJ: P&R Publishing, 2001.

———. *Reformed Dogmatics*. Edited and Translated by Richard B. Gaffin Jr. 5 vol. Bellingham, WA: Lexham Press, 2012–14.

Waltke, Bruce K., with Cathi J. Fredericks, *Genesis: A Commentary*. Grand Rapids: Zondervan, 2001.

Walton, John H. *The Lost World of Adam and Eve: Genesis 2–3 and the Human Origins Debate*. Downers Grove, IL: IVP Academic, 2015.

———. *The Lost World of Genesis One: Ancient Cosmology and the Origins Debate*. Downers Grove, IL: IVP Academic, 2009.

Waters, Guy Prentiss, J. Nicholas Reid, and John R. Muether, eds. *Covenant Theology: Biblical, Theological, and Historical Perspectives*. Wheaton, IL: Crossway, 2020.

Wenham, Gordon J. *Genesis 1–15*. Word Biblical Commentary. Grand Rapids: Zondervan, 1987.

Young, E. J. *The Book of Isaiah*. 3 vol. Grand Rapids: Eerdmans, 1972.